A DISCIPLE'S JOURNEY

Other Books by Dale Christensen

Patriot's Path (2014)
– a plan for our future

Dark Horse Candidate (2014)
– autobiography

Guide to Greatness (2014)
– inspiration to bring out the greatness in everyone

Thoughts in Verse (2014)
– uplifting poetry

10 Secrets To Speaking English (2001)
– method of helping people to speak a new language

Out of Print:

The Shopping Center Acquisition Handbook (1984)
– complete process and documentation

Turning the Hearts Vol. I-IV (*1982*)
– family history from earliest ancestors to marriage

History of the Church in Peru (1991)
– selective personal and general highlights

Entrepreneur Guide: The Ultimate Business & Learning Experience (2001)
– textbook for MBA course

Teaching Improvement Program
– *USTC MBA Program & Business School* (2001)
– training for MBA professors

A DISCIPLE'S JOURNEY

BY

Dale Christensen

A Disciple's Journey

Published by:
Dale Christensen
Books@Dale2016.com

Cover design: Matt Christensen and Rachael Gibson
Editing Assistance: Jan Jackson and Susan Allen Myers

Library of Congress, Catalog-in-Publication Data

ISBN
Hardback: 978-1-942345-12-1
Softback: 978-1-942345-13-8
eBook: 978-1-942345-14-5
Audio: 978-1-942345-15-2

Printed in the United States of America
Year of first printing: 2014

Dedication

This book is dedicated to my Savior and His prophets ,and to my parents and grandparents who inspired me to hear and accept the word of God and to be obedient to His commandments. And, to my loving and patient Sunday School and Primary teachers who didn't give up on me. And to my friends and missionary companions who tutored me. To those who believed on my words and trusted in my testimony of truth. To those who called me to serve and those who served with me. Finally, to my wife and children who are far better disciples than I am. I am grateful to have had the opportunity to be a disciple of Jesus Christ.

Table of Contents

Part I

Personal and Family

MISSION STATEMENTS, VALUES, AND GOALS

1. **I plan for the welfare of Zion:** I am a patriarch in my home. I am a pro-active leader and teacher in my church and community. I am a patriot and defend truth, freedom, and justice, and worship Jesus Christ as the God of this world. I see America as a promised and blessed land. I deem the Declaration of Independence and uphold the United States Constitution as inspired from God. I maintain that governments and laws are essential, and together with their citizens have sacred duties. I watch for and warn others of evil powers trying to destroy liberty.

2. **I have great worth:** I am faithful, humble, prayerful, righteous, and consecrate all that I have to God to build up His Kingdom on earth. I do good always and accomplish my foreordained mission and purpose and receive the blessings promised to Abraham, Isaac and Jacob. I do not fear making mistakes. I am sincere and decisive and repent of my sins, learn from my errors and practice self-mastery by controlling my desires, appetites and passions. I have faith and resist temptation. I enjoy life and endure to the end. I like myself, have inner peace, harmony and balance and endure all things. I relax and am of good cheer and have a sense of humor. I accept and adapt to all of life's challenges and opportunities and empathize with others. I leave a history of my life's experience for my posterity.

3. **I am honest in all my dealings:** I hold honesty and integrity as the premiere virtues and qualities of character for happiness in life and developing relationships and working with others.

4. **I am physically fit:** I appropriately nourish my body and I engage in appropriate exercise and physical work. I retire to bed early and rise early. I practice personal hygiene and I am well groomed and modestly dressed.

5. **I search for, live by and teach correct principles:** I search for truth and am teachable and always learn to develop my talents in order to prosper and assist others. I exercise faith and have a positive attitude. I think noble, benevolent, pure and virtuous thoughts. I think good of all people. I nourish and exercise my mind through all media. I am tolerant, open minded and non-judgmental, and I listen to and hear all perspectives and teach by the Spirit. I use my patriarchal blessings as a guide to my thoughts and actions.

6. **I practice excellence and produce quality:** I am successful in what I do through initiative, innovation, planning and discipline. I learn to do by doing and benefit from my experiences. I work hard and smart to accomplish meaningful goals. I am focused, industrious and take advantage of opportunities and do not procrastinate. I value and practice both specialization and diversification.

7. **I am a wise steward:** I make a positive difference in the world by seeking divine assistance and wise counsel from to help make decisions, develop talents and manage resources. My wants are subject to my needs and means. I invest wisely to increase the value and strength of my assets. My homestead is a source of increase. I have sufficient insurance and assets to meet the needs of my family in the event of

emergency, illness or death. My estate planning and business affairs are in order for my family or associates to continue in my absence. I have sufficient emergency food, fuel, clothing and money for my family's needs in case of emergency including savings for missions and education.

8. **I am financially independent:** I dedicate all that I have to God to help further His purposes. Money is my servant and I use it to accomplish good things. I increase my ability to earn through additional study and experience. I spend less than I earn and I invest and save some of all I earn. I am free of debt; own my own home, lands and precious possessions.

9. **I am environmentally aware:** I practice personal and environmental protection, order, comfort and improvement. I am living a long life and I have good health in old age with a body capable of service. I value natural resources, minimize pollution and don't waste.

My Mission Statement

Bring to pass the immortality and eternal life of man.

My Governing Values

1. **I love Heavenly Father:** I love and worship God. I learn his plan for me and receive personal revelation to strengthen my testimony.

2. **I am a disciple of Jesus Christ:** I live by and share Christ's teachings. I follow Christ's example. I follow the leaders of his church. I magnify my priesthood, and I am obedient to my priesthood leaders. I am active in the restored Church of Jesus Christ of Latter-day Saints. I use my free agency and the knowledge of truth to choose good over evil.

3. **I love my wife:** I am a faithful, loving, and courteous companion and my wife's best friend. I am understanding and always give her the benefit of the doubt. I inspire, build and cheer her spirit. I have daily companionship prayers and scripture study with her. I have regular planning sessions and personal priesthood interviews with her. My home is a bit of heaven on earth.

4. **I love my family:** I am a patriarch in my home. I am a devoted father and recognize my children as a crowning influence in my life. I foster family involvement that allows all of us to develop family closeness and a balance in work and lifestyle. I provide valuable experiences that allow my children to earn an inheritance.

5. **I love my fellowman:** I am a good son, brother and friend. I associate with good people and enjoy the good society of others. I love and appreciate the cultures and traditions of all people. I help others achieve their goals. I develop and strengthen positive relationships with others through friendship, courtesy, trust and teamwork. I communicate information and feelings in a timely and appropriate manner.

6. **I plan for the welfare of Zion:** I am a patriot and defend truth, freedom and justice. I see America as a promised and blessed land. I deem the Declaration of Independence and the United States Constitution as inspired from God. I maintain that governments and law are essential, and together with their citizens, have sacred duties. I watch for and warn others of evil powers trying to destroy liberty.

7. **I have great worth:** I am faithful, humble, prayerful, righteous, and consecrate all that I have to God to build up his kingdom on earth. I do good always and accomplish

my foreordained mission and purpose and receive the blessings promised to Abraham, Isaac and Jacob. I do not fear making mistakes. I am sincere and decisive. I repent of my sins, learn from my errors and practice self-mastery by controlling my desires, appetites and passions. I have faith. I like myself, have inner peace, harmony, and balance, and endure all things. I enjoy life. I am of good cheer and have a sense of humor. I relax. I accept and adapt to life's challenges and opportunities. I empathize with others. I am leaving a history of my life's experience for my posterity.

8. **I am honest in all my dealings:** I hold honesty and integrity as the premiere virtues and qualities of character for happiness and vital in developing relationships and working with others.

9. **I am physically fit:** I appropriately nourish my body, and I engage in appropriate exercise and physical work. I retire to bed early and rise early. I practice personal hygiene, and I am well groomed and modestly dressed. I am living a long life and I have good health in old age, with a body capable of service.

10. **I search for and live by correct principles:** I search for truth. I am teachable and develop my talents in order to prosper and assist others. I exercise faith and have a positive attitude. I think noble, benevolent, pure and virtuous thoughts. I think the best of all people. I nourish and exercise my mind through media. I am tolerant, open minded, and non-judgmental, and I listen to and hear all perspectives and teach by the Spirit. I use my patriarchal blessings as a guide to my thoughts and actions.

11. **I practice excellence and produce quality:** I am successful in what I do through initiative, innovation,

planning and discipline. I learn to do by doing and benefit from my experiences. I work hard and smart to accomplish meaningful goals. I am focused, industrious and take advantage of opportunities. I do not procrastinate. I value and practice both specialization and diversification.

12. **I am a wise steward:** I make a positive difference in the world by seeking Divine assistance and wise counsel to help make decisions, develop talents and manage resources. My wants are subject to my needs and means. I invest wisely to increase the value and strength of my assets. My homestead is a source of increase. I have sufficient insurance and assets to meet the needs of my family in the event of emergency, illness or death. My estate planning and business affairs are in order so that my family or associates could continue in my absence. I have sufficient food, fuel, clothing and money for my family's needs in case of emergency.

13. **I am financially independent:** I dedicate all that I have to God to help further his purposes. Money is my servant, and I use it to accomplish good things. I increase my ability to earn through additional study and experience. I spend less than I earn, and I invest and save some of all I earn. I am free of debt; own my own home, lands and precious possessions.

14. **I am environmentally aware:** I practice personal and environmental protection, order, comfort and improvement. I value natural resources, minimize pollution, and don't waste.

Christensen Family Constitution

Sherman, Connecticut – December 25, 1989

1. **We are a Christ-centered family**. We focus on individual and family spiritual welfare as the most important aspect

of being an eternal family. We are disciples of Christ, and we follow him. We learn of him, speak of him, worship the Father through him, and try to be like him.

2. **We are a united family**. We love one another and put our family ahead of other things. We always support each other and want to do activities together. We are different and unique in a very special way.

3. **We are a good family**. We are nice, kind, sweet and courteous. We are a serving, helpful, caring family. We do for others what they cannot do for themselves. We are a sharing and giving family and love others. We are a missionary family and strive to be a good example to others.

4. **We are a well-rounded family**. We are wise stewards in managing our time, talents, resources and assets. We are happy and fun loving. We are intelligent and stimulating and always seeking for truth. We value knowledge and learning. We continually explore all of God's creations, man's inventions, and the arts. We are healthy and active. We are neat and orderly. We are international, cosmopolitan, hometown and country.

5. **We are a patriotic family**. We love freedom and obey the law. We respect the rights, property and ideas of others. We are well informed of current events and historical facts. We are active in the political process and strive to defend freedom and justice.

6. **We are a prosperous family**. We are financially independent. We are free of debt and own our own home, land and precious possessions. We work together to save and invest for the future. We are self-sufficient and prepare for disaster with home storage, insurance, investments, assets and estate planning.

Lifetime Goals

A. Personal

1. Have a close and personal relationship with Heavenly Father and personally know Jesus Christ.
2. Have my calling and election made sure (the Second Comforter) and be worthy of ministering angels.
3. Receive a remission of my sins and be purified and sanctified by the power of the Holy Ghost.
4. Endure to the end and qualify to live in the highest degree of the Celestial Kingdom.
5. Have charity, or the pure love of Christ, for all people.
6. Receive inspiration and revelation for my personal needs and stewardships.
7. Keep an updated journal and write my life history.
8. Continue to be spiritually, physically and emotionally fit.
9. Be a strong, spiritual person who prays, studies, plans and follows through after thought and mediation and is obedient to my priesthood leaders.
10. Be a faithful and loving husband who is polite, courteous, understanding, cheerful, inspiring, romantic, and a best friend and companion.
11. Be a helping and loving father who guides by example.
12. Be a loyal friend and neighbor who helps and inspires others to strive for excellence.
13. Know and love family, friends and church members.

14. Help and motivate others by example, fellowship, and deed.

B. Marriage

1. Have our marriage sealed by the Holy Spirit of Promise.
2. Be a unified, happy, loving and romantic companionship.
3. Be the best of friends.
4. Enjoy a long, prolific, and progressive earth life, and plan for eternity together.

C. Family

1. Have a large family, with children serving church missions, marrying in the temple, and graduating from college. Be multilingual and well-rounded in the arts, sciences, business, social graces, and politics.
2. Travel and live worldwide.
3. Work together, do business together, and have fun together.
4. Keep a happy, harmonious and clean home.
5. Teach family members to respect one another and know how to be responsible, work hard, and be wise.
6. Family members should be self-sufficient and prepared for crisis and opportunities.

D. Church

1. Magnify priesthood and other callings and always be willing to serve and support church leaders.
2. Bring many unto Christ through testimony, example, faith and good works.

3. Preach the Gospel in the world and baptize many unto repentance.

4. Do an extraordinary amount of genealogy and temple work.

5. Help to build up the New Jerusalem and help gather the ten lost tribes.

6. Know church leadership and understand church programs.

E. Political

1. Be a strong influence for good, truth, freedom and justice.

2. Be well informed on current events, issues, historical facts, philosophies and prophecies.

3. Develop trusting and lasting relationships.

4. Be active in chosen political organizations.

5. Hold public offices of service, and support others in theirs.

F. Professional

1. Develop lasting relationships and respect among my associates.

2. Acquire additional credentials, experience and education to be of service and to achieve excellence.

3. Become an expert in my field of work. Write, teach and assist others by using my knowledge and skills.

G. Financial

1. Always happily pay tithes and offerings.

2. Own our home, lands, and precious possessions, and be free of debt
3. Be financially independent by living off income from investments.
4. Teach my family and others sound financial values, principles, and practices, and help them prosper and be independent.

Part II

What I Believe;
What I know

INTRODUCTION

"You can no more give what you ain't got
than go back to where you ain't been."
--Vermont Farmer

This book is a summary of many observations, principles I believe, and other things I know to be true. By sharing these, I feel a responsibility to do so in the right way and with an invitation for you, the reader, to find out for yourself if what I say is something you want to come to know for yourself.

To *believe* and to *know* are quite different. We can *believe* and accept many things, but it is different to *know* something. We can understand many things that are false, partially false, true, or partially true. But, to really know something, it must be *true.* What do you believe, and what do you know for sure?

Truth

It's important to tell the truth. It is a truth that different people perceive the truth depending on their personal perspectives and experiences, as described in the experience of the six blind men feeling various parts of an elephant. Each described what an elephant is by what they could feel with their hands.

If we tell the truth, we feel good about ourselves. If we lie, we feel bad and eventually begin to believe in our own lies. We all have our own perception of truth, but we also all know that there is a lot "out there" that we still need to experience in order to have all truth.

The following is a poem I wrote during the summer after I graduated from Boston College while working at Anthony's Pier 4 Restaurant in Boston. While waiting on a table of businessmen who had flown up to Boston from New York City to have lunch, I overheard one of them emphatically state, "It doesn't matter how you cut it, an apple is still an apple!" It really made an impression on me. The poem goes like this:

An Apple Is an Apple

An apple is an apple, no matter what the way
You choose to eat or cut it, or the price you have to pay.
It may be green and bitter, or very sweet and red.
It may be large and shiny or withered, small and dead.

You can carve that apple nicely or just leave it there to rot.
You can bake it in the oven, or stew it in a pot.
You can share it with a neighbor and make a real friend.
It's what you do with it that matters in the end.

Now truth is like that apple, it's very plain to see,
If it's in your hand at present or in a distant tree.
So hold to the fruit of wisdom, and seek the simple truth;
For wherever it may be found, the truth is still the truth.

1.

WHAT DO YOU BELIEVE, AND WHY?

"To be or not to be, that is the question."
--William Shakespeare

To Believe

To believe is to have confidence in or assume something to be true. It includes understanding that idea, event or person and consciously making a decision to accept it as reality. When we do this, our perception of the world or the rest of reality will be influenced by this decision or belief. It is as though we choose to put on a pair of tinted sun glasses. All we now see is colored by that tint.

Some call it our *belief window*. We put beliefs on our belief window and react to the world based on what is on that window. For example, if we believe that all dogs are mean and vicious; then when we see a dog, we will feel fear, shrink, or run. On the other hand, if we believe all dogs are friendly and looking for love and attention; then when we see a dog, we will feel love, hold out our hand and move toward it. In reality, each individual dog may be somewhere in between these two descriptions.

Nevertheless, we have a choice as to what we will accept and believe regardless of what the reality may be. We can choose to believe that all dogs are friendly and looking for love and attention even though we know that some may be dangerous.

It is our choice that will determine how we act or react. It is our choice that will help us gain knowledge and come to know reality as it was, as it is, and as it is to be.

To Know

We can know reality by observing, studying and experimenting. Most knowledge comes from our senses. Unless they are handicapped, most people have the five physical senses of sight, smell, hearing, taste and touch. Every person also has a sixth sense of spirit, or feeling of the heart. Our brain processes and evaluates the experiences of all these senses and allows us to think, make choices and act or react.

There's an ancient proverb that goes like this:

He who knows not and knows not that he knows not, he is a fool, shun him.
He who knows not and knows that he knows not, he is simple, teach him.
He who knows and knows not that he knows, he is asleep, wake him.
He who knows and knows that he knows, he is wise; follow him.

To Testify

Depending on what we have experienced with our six senses, we make choices to *believe*, and then we can come to *know*. Throughout our life, we describe the world and our experiences as we believe or know them to be. We witness, or testify, as to what we have, what we do, what we are, and what we want, etc. This process is called giving a testimony. In a court of law, we are sworn to tell the truth, the whole truth and nothing but the truth, so help us God.

Very few of us are ever called up on the witness stand to place our hand on the Bible and swear this oath. However, we all give our testimony to ourselves or others every day. This is called bearing or baring testimony. There are two ways to spell the word. The commonly used word to bear a testimony is spelled "BEAR." According to the dictionary, it means:

1. To carry;
2. To have or to show (as it bore his signature);
3. To support or sustain; and
4. To supply (as to bear witness).

The other spelling is "BARE" which means to expose or to make known or visible; to reveal or uncover.

We all carry (bear) a testimony where ever we go and whatever we do.

We should also concentrate on uncovering, revealing and making visible (bare) our testimony.

2.

WHAT DO YOU KNOW FOR SURE?

"I think, therefore I am."
--Rene Descartes

We Exist

Philosophers and mathematicians may argue that the quote above is not logical and does not prove our existence. I disagree. I see. I hear. I smell. I taste. I touch. I feel in my being. I am, and I know you are, because all my senses confirm that you are also. More than anything, I feel empathy for you. I feel love for you and I know in my being that I am important, and that you are as important as I am.

There is nothing logical or scientific that can deny our existence or disprove who we are, where we came from before we were born, and where we are going after we die. On the contrary, logic and science are beginning to confirm what holy and wise men have been saying for centuries and even millennia. Even though we don't know all the answers right now, someday we will understand and be amazed at the simplicity of it all.

Divine Creator

To choose to disbelieve in a divine creator or in an eternal purpose is to choose to believe that the sun does not shine or warm the earth. To choose to believe that mankind, along with all forms of life and elements of the earth, came about by accident or chance is to choose to believe that books were written by an explosion in a print shop or a computer was created by lighting hitting a pond of petroleum and a copper mine.

Relationship and Purpose

People of all races, cultures and languages develop relationships in order to survive, propagate and find happiness, comfort and purpose. We observe all plant and animal life struggling to do the same, but there is a difference. Mankind searches for purpose and meaning in life. In addition to taking care of physical needs, they have a great desire and go to great effort to attend to divine spiritual needs. These desires and efforts include those who have lived before and those who will live after them. There is an advanced relationship and purpose to life for all people of the earth.

I Believe

I believe we are eternal beings, having a mortal experience on this earth. If we exist on this earth for a purpose, then it seems logical that there would be other planets in the universe that have been created for the same purpose. If there are other such planets, they would also have life forms similar to ours.

I Know

I know that I am a child of God and He loves me. I know that we are all brothers and sisters of an eternal family, God loves each of us, and has a plan for us to progress and be happy.

3.

OPPOSITION IN ALL THINGS

"For every action, there is an equal and opposite reaction."
--(Third Law) Sir Isaac Newton

History of Mankind

Throughout the recorded history of mankind, there has been a struggle between good and evil. I believe that good choices promote liberty and freedom, and evil choices limit or destroy liberty and freedom. Most human beings want to be free and want to help others be free.

When rights and freedoms have been respected and protected, the people have prospered and been happy. When they have been infringed upon or destroyed, there has been sadness, war, destruction, and death. The history of the world is a history of the struggle between freedom and slavery.

Governments and laws have always been established to protect rights and liberty. At the same time there have always been individuals, or groups of individuals, who have wanted to have power over others or to possess what others have. When any individual begins to have a little power, they want to have more and more power, until they dominate, or have power, over others. They can only do this by taking away the rights and freedom others have.

Good and Evil

If there is a God and we are his children, wouldn't it be logical that he would us establish governments and laws to protect liberty and freedom? If there is a God and he is good, would it not be logical that there is evil and those who promote evil? I choose to believe in God and in good. I also believe there is evil and those who promote evil.

I Know

I know that God has given mankind inalienable rights of life, liberty and the pursuit of happiness. I know that the freedom to choose our course of action is an eternal principle, and is essential for us to progress. I know that with this freedom comes responsibility. I know that we are not free to choose the *consequences* of our actions, whether good or bad. I know that they follow as a natural result of our choices.

4.

WHAT IS YOUR GOLDEN CALF?

Human Perception

The ancient parable of the six blind men and the elephant argues that unwise people deny various aspects of truth they don't understand. Misunderstanding results from partial truths or inaccurate perception. By considering all viewpoints, we can try to see the whole picture of reality. It is tempting and very easy to close our minds to additional light, facts, and knowledge, and to simply fill in the blanks with sweeping generalizations. We must beware that our five physical senses can be deceived.

The Blind Men and An Elephant

John Godfrey Saxe (1816-1887)

It was six men of Indostan to learning much inclined,
Who went to see the Elephant (Though all of them were blind),
That each by observation might satisfy his mind.

The First approached the Elephant, and happening to fall
Against his broad and sturdy side, at once began to bawl:
"God bless me! But the Elephant is very like a wall!"

The Second, feeling of the tusk, cried, "Ho! What have we here
So very round and smooth and sharp? To me 'tis mighty clear,
This wonder of an Elephant is very like a spear!"

The Third approached the animal, and happening to take
The squirming trunk within his hands, thus boldly up and spake:
"I see," quoth he, "the Elephant is very like a snake!"

The Fourth reached out an eager hand, and felt about the knee.
"What most this wondrous beast is like is mighty plain," quoth he;
"Tis clear enough the Elephant is very like a tree!"

The Fifth, who chanced to touch the ear, said: "E'en the blindest man
Can tell what this resembles most; deny the fact who can,
This marvel of an Elephant is very like a fan!"

The Sixth no sooner had begun about the beast to grope,
Than, seizing on the swinging tail that fell within his scope,
"I see," quoth he, "the Elephant is very like a rope!"

And so these men of Indostan disputed loud and long,
Each in his own opinion exceeding stiff and strong,
Though each was partly in the right, and all were in the wrong!

Moral:

So oft in theologic wars, the disputants, I ween,
Rail on in utter ignorance of what each other mean,
And prate about an Elephant not one of them has seen!

Divine Nature

If there is a God in Heaven, is it logical to conclude that he might make himself known to man? Would he not give us some indication of who he is and our relationship to him? If there is a God and we are related to him, would our nature be such that we could understand for what purpose we exist and for what destination we are bound? Why would he create this earth, and how did he put us here?

It seems logical that the answers to these questions should be simple and easy to understand. It also seems logical if there is effort to promote good, there is also effort to promote evil. As in any conflict, the opposing sides try to understand their enemy. There will be efforts to define and persuade their point of view through example, power and propaganda. There will also be efforts to expose the weaknesses of the enemy, scramble or destroy the lines of communication, and to confuse the combatants into thinking they may be on the wrong team.

In the Image of God

Perhaps it's not as important to understand how or when we arrived or were placed on this earth. Perhaps it's more important to understand *who we are* and *why we are here*. Holy men have written only sentences about the "how" and "when", but have written volumes to explain the "who" and the "why." Perhaps religious people will be just as surprised as the non-believers when they find the answers to these questions.

If there is a God and he were to create beings, would he not want to create something like unto himself? Would he create a place for these beings and the resources for them to survive? Would he create them and put them somewhere just to exist, or would he have a purpose? If there were a purpose, would he give these beings hints and helps along the way, or would he just give them all the tools, answers, and resources?

First Humans

There are a lot of theories about how the first man or woman or being came to live on earth. Many people have gone to great lengths to explain how things have come to be, with and without a God. None of these theories can be proved or explained in conclusive any detail. We are left to choose for ourselves what to believe.

I Believe

I believe that every person born into this world has an innate belief in a Supreme Being, or God. I also believe they all have a conscience, or inner compass, to recognize good from evil. From their childhood, they are taught to believe that God is such and such or believe that there is no god. This conditioning and their environment has a tremendous influence on their perceptions and beliefs. It also has a profound effect on how their conscience and inner compass works. However, at some point in everyone's life, each person chooses what they will believe. If someone is forced to believe or do something, they usually rebel.

Little by little, each person comes to believe in God and his or her purpose in life.

I know

I know that God lives and is our Heavenly Father who created our spirits. We are his children, and he loves each of us. We are part of a Heavenly Family. We chose Jesus Christ to be our leader and Savior. Jesus made it possible for us to overcome sin and death. The Holy Spirit communicates with our spirit to comfort us, guide us, and help us know truth from error.

5.

INTER-GALACTIC COMMUNICATION

Rituals

Almost every individual, family and community has rituals or ceremonies to define their culture, behavior or celebrations. Surely every religion has ceremonies and rituals for the same purpose.

Scientists and other enthusiasts speculate, hypothecate, and spend lots of time, energy, and money studying crop circles in local farm fields, along with distant stars and strange sounds from outer space. Are they answers to messages, or just echoes from messages sent yesterday or millennia ago? Regardless, it's becoming clearer and clearer, or at least more logical, that we are not alone in the universe.

Why should we be surprised if there are others wanting to investigate *us* or understand *us*? Are we the good guys needing to figure out how to defend ourselves from the monsters from outer space? Or, are we the bad guys who have done some pretty terrible things? Are space aliens wanting what we have, or do they want to protect themselves from us? I have no idea. But a reasonable person might ask, "If there are space aliens, who are they, what is their purpose, and what is our relationship to them?"

It's so easy to get distracted from that which is important. There is so much noise in the world that it is often difficult to hear the good music or the good news. In today's fast-paced world, long-established traditions and rituals are being replaced by momentary flashes of information and interest.

Prayer

Is there a way for us to stay tuned to that which is important and vital to our life and to the world? What would it be? If there is a God, would he not give us some kind of process to stay focused? Do we have a means of communication with the Almighty and we just don't know it or don't use it? Is that possible? Can anyone in the world have such communication? Most people in the world think so, even though there is a growing few who want to convince everyone otherwise. Is this the kind of opposition we can expect? Is this what evil is trying to do?

Can we get direction for our inner compass by just asking? Can we learn, come to understand, and then know truth by asking and then listening? Could it be just that simple? Would God deal this way with his creations if he really is there? If we asked, would he really answer? Can a person really know God this way, or is it just wishful thinking?

Prophets or Props

In his wisdom, would God choose certain people to give hints, knowledge, truth, or guidance for the rest of mankind? People from all over the world have looked to such holy men for guidance and for truth. If God did speak to prophets in olden times, how did so many different religions come to be? How did God's truth get changed and mixed up so there are so many explanations of God, the purpose of life, and explanation of where we came from, why we're here, and where we are going. Was evil always trying to confuse and divide people?

Scriptures or Scripts

Did these holy men record the truths they received for their day, for their posterity, and even for us? If they did, how did their writings make it through the centuries to end up in our hands and in our language?

Why don't all the ancient Holy Scriptures say the same thing in the same words or language? Why are there discrepancies or contradictions in their explanations or teachings? Did good men always rewrite or translate them as they came down through the ages? Did all the truths make it to us, or were there things left out or mistranslated? Common sense would suggest that it would be difficult to get exactly the same words and meaning to us through thousands of years and by way of many languages.

I Believe

I believe that people of all nations and religions feel closeness to one another as they worship their creator. They perform rituals and ceremonies to show their creator that they want to do the right thing and be happy. I believe these people worship the same god, but in different ways. I believe that each of their religions have some of the truth that God has given to his prophets over the centuries. However, there have been evil influences that have hidden or changed some of the truths in order to confuse and divide mankind.

I believe that people are sincere in their desire to do good, and most feel love for others and a need to help others. If there is discrimination or hatred, it is because of evil influences or actions of those trying to destroy faith in God or trying to rob people of their freedoms and self-esteem. I believe God hears and answers prayers of all his children regardless of their age, race or religion. He loves us all, and he wants us all to be happy.

I believe that holy writings are from God and that they are true unless they have been mistranslated or changed by evil influence or action. They are not scripts for us to act out, but they are guideposts for us to follow. I believe the purer they are, the more we can rely on them. I believe that God will judge people according to the light and knowledge they have. I also believe that every person will have the opportunity to receive all the light and knowledge God intends for them to have. I believe all people are equal before God, and will be blessed accordingly.

I know

I know that God has always spoken to his children through prophets. He also gave the prophets knowledge and power to act for him and to bless his children. Prophets are guides for us to follow. They have always written God's words in Holy Scriptures. I know that there are living prophets today, and I know the scriptures are true. I know that we can also communicate directly with God through prayer. We address him as Heavenly Father, thank him for what we have, ask him for what we need, in the name of Jesus Christ.

6.

STUCK IN A TIME WARP

Man's Nature

If we are offspring of God, then do we have his divine DNA, and can we become like him? Are our appetites, desires and passions attributes of God? Can they be developed into divine dimensions or distorted into carnal corruption? Are we left to choose for ourselves between good and evil, or do we just have to accept our fate?

Hero, Villain or Soap Opera

We are certain that everyone who is born will someday die. We are also certain that every person will make mistakes by choosing to do something evil. We all have this wonderful body that is beautiful in its youth, but weakens as it grows old. If there is a God, he must be magnificent, good and even perfect. Logic, along with the words of holy men, would demand that nothing imperfect could be in his presence. Is there a way to overcome sin and death, or are we stuck in a soap opera, where we keep making the same mistakes for eternity? Is there a hero to save us from sin and death? Is there a villain trying to distract us and keep us from rising to our potential?

May the Force Be with You

Almost every religion has a god or force that will make things right. There is someone or something that has the power, authority, or ability to overcome evil. Science fiction thinkers are projecting these images on screens. Are they accurate, or just another attempt to bolster the hopes of people that all is not lost, and that there is a bright future if we just hold on a little longer.

I Believe

I believe that most people around the earth have a desire to return to God and live with him forever. I believe that most people want to be saved from evil and suffering. They express it in different ways, but they hope for someone with power to rescue or save them from evil and doom.

I know

I know that we chose to follow Jesus Christ in our pre-mortal life and earned the right to have a physical body and gain experience. I know that Adam and Eve were given two commandments. They couldn't keep one without breaking the other. Adam sinned so we could gain bodies and be tested. We are responsible for our own sins and not for Adam's. Jesus was born of the Virgin Mary and lived a perfect life. He taught his Gospel, established his church, called his apostles, and gave them the authority to act for him. He suffered and died for us so we could overcome our sins and be resurrected.

7.

PAGAN, POMPOUS, PROPITIATION?

Religion

In years past, most people regarded religion as something sacred and holy. It was something to be respected by others of different religions, even though great wars and destruction were caused by those who used religion to gain wealth and power.

Today, many people are skeptical and view religion as something of a charade. Some feel that they have been duped, as their ancestors were duped, by religious leaders professing piety but really asking for money or power.

Ceremony

Was there once a true religion on the earth? If so, which religion was it, and where did it go, or what happened to it? Would God be a god of confusion and create many religions or churches? Could God be pleased to see the many religions and churches contending with one another? Is religion a lot of ceremony for spectators to watch, or is it something to participate in?

What does God think when one religion tries to dominate or destroy another? Were governments created to help protect individuals and families from this domination, as well as to protect the right to worship according to the dictates of their own consciences?

Hierarchy

Did God favor one people over another, and if so, why? Who are those favored people? Where are they, and how can one become favored with and like them?

If God had a religion or church, what would it look like? What would such a religion or church teach? How would it be organized, and how would it be funded? What would be the requirements to be part of such a religion or church, and how could one qualify to join?

A Dynamic Education

Logic and reason would suggest that if there was such a "true" religion or church, then it would be teaching a powerful message and invite all to participate. There would be definite and clear doctrine. There would be a clear organization and hierarchy for people to follow and participate in. It should be the closest thing to heaven than anything else. It should be the real thing that answers the tough questions and gives the peace and comfort people seek.

I Believe

I believe that God's true church would teach true religion and be the true organization with true doctrine and power. I believe it would have the "gifts of the spirit" and miracles by those who believe. I believe it would have prophets, apostles, pastors, evangelists, priests, bishops, teachers and deacon, etc. I believe it should have God's power and authority to do his will. I believe people could have a way to recognize it and join it if they chose to.

I know

I know that God is not a God of confusion. Jesus Christ established his church in ancient times with true doctrine, organization, and priesthood authority. He foretold that his church and the truths he taught would be lost during the dark ages. He promised to restore all things in the latter days. I know he has restored his true church in these last days with his doctrine, organization and priesthood authority. I have been blessed to receive this priesthood. My priesthood line of authority is as follows:

DALE H CHRISTENSEN was ordained a High Priest April 10, 1983 by Thomas B. Kerr.

THOMAS B. KERR was ordained a High Priest March 16, 1958 by George Q. Morris.

GEORGE Q. MORRIS was ordained an Apostle April 8, 1954 by David O. McKay.

DAVID O. MCKAY was ordained an Apostle April 9, 1906 by Joseph F. Smith.

JOSEPH F. SMITH was ordained an Apostle July 1, 1866 by Brigham Young.

BRIGHAM YOUNG was ordained an Apostle February 14, 1835 under the hands of the Three Witnesses, Oliver Cowdery, David Whitmer and Martin Harris.

The THREE WITNESSES were called by revelation to choose the Twelve Apostles and on February 14, 1835, were "blessed by the laying on of hands of the Presidency," Joseph Smith, Jr., Sidney Rigdon and Frederick G. Williams, to ordain the Twelve Apostles.

JOSEPH SMITH JR. and OLIVER COWDERY received the Melchizedek Priesthood in 1829 under the hands of Peter, James, and John.

PETER, JAMES, and JOHN were ordained Apostles by the Lord Jesus Christ. (New Testament; John 15:16)

8.

PRINCIPLES AND PROMISES

Superstition

If faith is hope in something that is true, but is not seen, what is superstition? Is superstition a counterfeit of faith? If there is truth about God, are there lies about him? If there are true prophets, are there also false prophets, and how do you know the difference? Should we try to have faith that we can become better and ultimately realize our full potential? If so, how do we do this?

Chemical Reactions

If we make dramatic changes in our life by accepting religion and its doctrine, will we experience a physical change in our bodies, or is it only a change in our spirit body? When we are born again, do we actually experience a physical phenomenon?

With a spiritual rebirth, do we undergo a psychological change, and what happens to our physical DNA? Are we the same person, or are we a different person?

Extra-Terrestrial Communication

With faith and a mighty change of heart and expression of commitment through baptism, is there an actual gift from God to help us along our way? If the Holy Spirit manifested itself on the Day of Pentecost in the New Testament, would the only true church today also have these gifts of the spirit? Is the change a one-time event, or is it something that needs to be renewed or refreshed? How is that done?

I Believe

I believe that when people choose to believe and do something about it, they are exercising faith. When they do this, they actually experience a mighty change of heart and soul. People of many religions and churches experience this and make commitments to God to dedicate their lives to him. I believe that God loves them as much as he loves me. I believe that the Holy Spirit is manifested in the lives of people who seek, ask, and knock. I believe that God works through many people, many religions and many churches. There is no monopoly on truth or righteous living. However, I believe he also works through his designated representatives to whom he has given his authority.

I know

I know that faith is the eternal principle that helps us to become like Jesus Christ. Repentance is the process of change from doing evil things to doing Godly things. Baptism allows us to be clean and begin a new life as though we were born again or raised from the dead. With baptism we can be confirmed a member of Christ's true church and be given a special gift called the Gift of the Holy Ghost. With this gift comes the "gifts of the Spirit."

9.

CATALYSTS OR CONTAGIOUS?

What's Your Yoga?

Is there a time for everything including work and rest? Is there a time for eating and refraining from eating and drinking? What is your formula for rejuvenating your mind, body and spirit? Regardless of your beliefs about religion, do you believe you need to rest once in a while? Do you believe that God had giving us a hint for healthy and happy living by commanding us to work six days and rest every seventh day?

Eat, Drink, and Be Merry

Scientists prescribe a periodic cleansing fast to help purify our blood and renew our vital organs. Do you believe this, and do you do it? If you do, how often do you do it? Do you refrain from food *and drink,* or just food? When you fast, do you refrain from other activities? Do you do it for only physical reasons, or are there other reasons you fast? What are they?

Dirt, Sweat, and Bread

The Bible says that we should work six days in seven and earn our bread by the sweat of our brow. There are a lot of ways to work and sweat. How do you interpret this? Do you think working is an honorable and necessary thing to do? Have you learned to love hard work and work hard at the things you love? Or, is work just something you have to do to get money? Do you just trade your time for money, or do you put your heart and soul into your work? Are you happy with what you do and how you do it?

Getting Lost to Find Your Way

Is it possible to find yourself by losing yourself in serving others? Does the "Golden Rule" really work to make life better for all, and do you live it? If you believe in the Golden Rule and live it, how does it affect your daily actions?

I Believe

I believe every person, animal and machine needs to rest occasionally. I believe people develop strength through discipline and conquering their appetites, desires and passions. I believe honest work is the best medicine for happy living. I believe humans becomes more humane when treating others with dignity and kindness.

I know

I know that God has commanded us to work six days and rest on the seventh. He expects us to take responsibility for our thoughts and actions and to care for and love others. We can develop this love by serving others.

10.

PRACTICES AND CONDITIONING

Veggies and Vitamins

Is there any doubt in your mind that there are certain things you should and should not take into your body? Do you understand that eating or drinking good things to excess may endanger your health? Do you believe that your body is different from ever one else's body, and that you can sense if your body needs a little fine tuning?

Fountain of Feelings

Is it possible for you to love someone else more than yourself? If you do, is that a good thing? Will such love cause you to promote what is best for the other person? Is it enough to just occasionally give something to those in need, or is it better to invest yourself, too?

Straight Talk

Is it true that "It's a tangled web we weave, if first we practice to deceive?" We've been told, "If you're going to talk the talk, then you need to walk the walk." Why is it important for our actions to be congruent with our thoughts and words? If they are all not congruent or in alignment, are we really being honest? What can we do to bring them into alignment? Are you completely honest with others and with yourself?

Tithing and Tribute

Why do so many religions and churches teach that we should offer a tribute or a tithing for the poor? If there is a God, does he need our money? Can't he take care of these less-fortunate people? Why would he ask us to give something we have to help someone who doesn't have? What is the purpose of doing this, and who benefits the most?

I Believe

I believe that most people want to be healthy and take good care of their bodies. However, many people have been deceived by evil influences to eat and drink products that are harmful. I believe that many artificial substances are harmful, and many natural substances can be harmful if not used properly.

I believe that most people love others and are willing to serve others when needed. Most people try to be honest, but many are dishonest from time to time. I believe that if people pay their tithes and offerings they will receive the blessings from heaven, even if the funds might sometimes be used incorrectly.

I know

I know that our bodies are creations of God, and we should treat them with care and respect. I know that charity is the pure love of Christ, and we feel it by loving and serving others. I know we can learn to become like God and inherit all that he has by living his commandments and generously giving of tithes and offerings.

11.

FORMULAS FOR EVOLUTION

Private or Public Information

If there is a God and he gave truth and vital information for us to succeed in life, is it private or public information? Who should have access to it, and who should interpret it? If we have it, do we have a responsibility to share it? If we don't have it, do we have a responsibility to look for it? What should I be doing with the truth I have? What should you be doing with the truth you have?

Return on Investment (ROI)

How many years, during our life on earth, do we have an opportunity to develop our natural talents and to improve our skills? How can I know what my talents are, and the best way to improve my skills? If I do a good job and really magnify myself, will I be better off in the next life? What about those who don't understand this, or who don't have the opportunities that I have?

The Scientific Method

Are there both *physical* and *spiritual* laws of the universe that govern the universe itself and everything in it? If these laws are followed or obeyed, will there be a specific result or benefit? If they are not obeyed, will there be an opposite result or consequence?

Can these laws be tested and proven? Who knows and understands these laws? Where can they be found, and were can the benefits or consequences be understood and realized? What is the process of gathering the empirical data, analyzing and interpreting it, and how are these findings shared?

I Believe

I believe there are truths, and if we have them we should share them with others. I believe that most people want to do this and many try, but there are evil influences discouraging this practice. I believe that people all over the world rise above their surroundings to exceed great heights. There are also many people who are given much, but neglect to build upon or share what they have. I believe this is the biggest waste of humanity. I believe that people who obey or disobey universal laws are rewarded or punished accordingly.

I know

I know that the truths I hold to be self-evident are of great value, and I have a responsibility and opportunity to share them with everyone. I know we can develop innate talents we brought with us from before we were born. We can develop skills through prayer, effort and persistence. I know that God's commandments are guides to help us be successful and happy. Obedience to his commandments is an eternal law by which we receive eternal blessings.

12.

TRIBES AND TITLES

Forever Yours

Is there a reason we were born into a certain family or set of circumstances? Is our birth a random thing, or something we were assigned or chose to do? Are friendships or family relations only temporary, or can they last beyond this life. Is a relationship between a husband and a wife different than a relationship between parents and child?

What about dear friendships? Can relationships last forever? If not, what is the purpose of all this anyway? Is there a proper or improper way to behave and cultivate relationships? If so, what are the ways?

Benefits and Responsibilities

Just because I'm a member of a family, do I have to like it? Do I have to contribute to the family, or can I just endure it? What about you? What kinds of relationships do you have? What kind of relationships to you want? What are you doing to foster and develop the healthy relationships you want?

If I really love someone today and we get married, how is it possible to dislike her next year? What kind of love does it take to have the kind of love that won't allow this to happen? What else is needed to make sure that our relationships will not end when we or others die? Will we see our loved ones again after this life? If so, what will be our relationship there? What is the purpose of a relationship there?

Is having sex and making babies just to perpetuate the species, or is there more to it? If there is more to it, what is it, and why are sexual relations and emotions so complex? Why can't people just have safe sex and be happy? Why are the sexual norms changing so rapidly during the past decades?

I Believe

I believe that people all over the world seek for and cherish relationships with others. I believe people all over the world hold marriage and family sacred.

I know

I know that marriage between a man and a woman is ordained of God. The family is vital as the basic unit on earth and in eternity. I know that love can be eternal, with marriages solemnized by God's sealing power. Individuals must not have sexual relations with anyone who is not their legally wedded spouse. In order to enjoy lasting love and happiness, husbands and wives must be completely faithful to each other. The Law of Chastity was given in the beginning and is still in force for those who are single or married. Those who break the Law of Chasity must repent or suffer the consequences of their thoughts and actions.

13.

ANCESTOR WORSHIP

Dry Bones

Dem dry bones were written of by Ezekiel and sung about by many. Just how many bones have there been on the earth? How many people have actually lived on the earth? Scientists don't agree on how many billions of people have been born, nor the length of time humans have occupied this earth. Needless to say, there have been a lot!

We all have many, many ancestors, and we are all related if we go back far enough in our genealogy. There have been many civilizations that have flourished and then died out. Their stories have pretty much been lost through history. What happened to them? What are all those people doing now?

Live Bones

There are approximately seven billion people living on the earth today. You and I are two of that number. We live in a magnificent time of technology, knowledge, and advancement. We have an opportunity to learn, travel and become whatever we want. Well, some of us can do that, but a lot of people don't have the opportunity or the means to.

What are we doing to help other people have what we have and know what we know? What will happen to them if we never get through to them?

Dem Bones

If God exists and if he is our Heavenly Father, would he give some of his children a chance to return and live with him, but deny others just because they didn't know about him?

If there is a God, is he a just and merciful God? Would he not love all of his children, and would he not provide a just and merciful plan for them all to have an opportunity to return to live with him? Logic would suggest that if such a being existed, and if we were created by him, then it would have to be so.

But, why is there so much poverty? Why is there so much suffering? Why is there so much war and evil? It seems logical that we all came to earth for a purpose. It's reasonable to assume that gaining a physical body and having a mortal experience is ultimately good for our spirit, regardless of what kind of body or experience we have. It's comforting to know that the body will ultimately be among "dem bones," but that our spirit lives on.

I Believe

I believe that people all over the world today love their children, just as their ancestors did. I believe that most religions believe and teach that there is a link between us and our ancestors. Some religions go farther than others to relate to and even worship their ancestors.

I believe that the true knowledge of our relationship to our ancestors has been on the earth among many groups of people, but this understanding has been confused or lost because of evil influences. Traditions and beliefs have been passed down and are expressed in different ways around the world.

I know

I know that God is both just and merciful. He will give every one of his children the opportunity to become like him even if they did not have the opportunity to hear or take advantage of his plan in this life. We have the opportunity and obligation to do for our dead ancestors what they cannot do for themselves. We can go to the House of the Lord (a temple) and be baptized, endowed and sealed for those who did not have the opportunity to take advantage of these sacred ordinances while they lived on the earth. I know our ancestors and loved ones are alive in spirit. They are anxious for us to provide these ordinances for them as they await their resurrection. Everyone who has ever lived will be so blessed.

14.

FINAL EXAMINATION

Report Card

It has been said the only things that are certain are "death and taxes." However, some people don't pay taxes. The only certain things for each individual are "birth, experience, and death." Our experiences will vary widely depending on our family, opportunities, environment, and geography.

We will all die. So, when we die, where do we go? What do we do there? What do we lose or get? Are we punished or rewarded? Is death like a graduation? Do we get a report card? If so, what are we graded on, and what does the grade mean?

Graduate School

If there is a God and we are his children, do we just stop learning and go home to sing songs and say nice things about God? Do we just sit around and be happy that we made it, or sad that we didn't? Was our short time living on this earth in Paris or on a tiny jungle island all there is?

If there is a God, and he wants us to progress to be like him, would he have additional learning experiences planned for us? Is there a post-graduate educational opportunity available? What is it, and what are the requirements to apply and be accepted? What is the tuition? What specialty are we going to study?

Diploma and Degree

Every person who has been born has done something worth merit, even if it was just to gain a body. If there is a God, would he have a plan to give some kind of reward for every person who made it through earth life? Is it just a diploma or a certificate of accomplishment? Do we get an associate's degree for having lived? Do we get a bachelor's degree in knowledge, influence, fame, or fortune?

Would a true God reward his children according to their circumstances or according to what they did with their circumstances? Would every person receive the same diploma? Will we have a chance to participate in deciding our own grade? What were the expectations of our earthly learning experiences? What was the course curriculum, and what are the deadlines for turning in our papers and projects? Can we get extra credit? Is it possible to cheat on the daily tests or on the final exam? Come on! Please, what are the correct answers? Better yet, what are the right questions?

I Believe

I believe every person in the world knows with a certainty that his or her life has purpose and meaning. I believe that our choices and beliefs will develop or diminish our understanding of that purpose and meaning. I believe that all people are here on this earth to learn and grow. Not everyone will have an equal opportunity on this earth, but everyone will have a fair and equal opportunity to learn the entire curriculum and receive the highest grade possible. I believe that all people want to do well, succeed, and pass the test. I believe that all people desire, and most know in their minds and hearts, that they are responsible for their own actions and ultimate grade and reward.

I know

I know that I will be judged according to my thoughts, desires, and actions. If I am faithful to God's teachings and endure to the end, I will receive a reward or glory equal to my qualifications. God will do anything to help me progress and qualify to live with him and inherit the exalted life he lives. He will help me judge and receive a just reward. I want to be like God, my Heavenly Father, and I know I can if I do my part.

15.

THE LAST WORD

The Last Word

It is my sincere desire that you understand what I believe and what I know. I realize that you may have different beliefs and may doubt some of what I have written. I invite you to consider what I have said. I invite you to make a decision to believe what I believe and ask God with a sincere heart and humble spirit if it is true. If you do this, I promise you that you will realize beautiful things in your life that you may have never considered before. If you choose not to seek, ask, or knock, then we can still be friends and respect each other for the good people we are trying to be.

Thank you for your time and for reading my book. It is my hope that you find the happiness you seek and to make good choices that will determine your own destiny. May God bless and keep you and your loved ones.

If you want to learn more or discuss what you have read with someone, I recommend you look at the following two websites: Mormon.org and LDS.org. For specific topics, you can also find The *Encyclopedia of Mormonism* online.

In addition to reading the Bible (King James Version), I invite you to read the Book of Mormon, the Doctrine & Covenants, and the Pearl of Great Price. You can find both text and voice recordings on the web sites above.

Part III

Articles on a Variety of Topics

1.

A FIRM'S GREATEST ASSET? WORKERS

Employees can be an entrepreneur's biggest challenge and his greatest asset. Some say it is a "dog eat dog world" or "survival of the fittest" and all that stuff. However, valued employees will be there for you when you need them. They can perform in your presence and cover for you in your absence. Sure, you may be taken advantage of on occasion, but that will be the exception rather than the rule.

Treat your employees right. They help entrepreneurs succeed. Owners are like the tip of the iceberg that rises above the water line to brave the cold wind or bask in the warm sunshine. Employees represent the unseen mass that keeps their employer above water, supporting and making it all possible.

Occasionally, inexperienced entrepreneurs may "hold back" top employees from promotions because of a fear of losing them. We all remember the good teachers in our lives. They gave us the tools, skills and opportunities to excel and then pushed us to do our best. Employers play the same role in the lives of those who work with them.

Employee service should come ahead of customer service. In fact, employees are our most valuable customers. A good employer will train and develop employees so they will become valuable contributors. It should be taken as a compliment if they go on to do bigger and better things, hopefully in your company.

Employee turnover can be fatal and is one of the biggest costs in doing business. Some companies with high turnover seem to have an attitude of "turn and burn"! They go through many new employees, who finally get fed up and go elsewhere. Other very successful companies have zero or very low turnover by providing fair salaries, benefits and training.

"Average" is the best of the worst and the worst of the best. To get the best, pay the best. If you pay minimum wages, you can expect minimum results. Sadly, many employers also keep employees working only part-time so the employer doesn't have to provide benefits.

Bill Walton of Walmart wouldn't stand for this. Hyrum Smith of Franklin Cove, tells the story of paying his receptionist top salary. He believed that the most valuable employee was the one that the outside world speaks to first.

Older and more mature employees should not be overlooked. Someone with experience and gray hair may be stable and valuable. Many stores hire older employees who want to work and who know how to treat customers right.

Wise entrepreneurs will have good protective systems in place, but they will trust their employees. They know if they have faith in their employees instead of fear, the employees will respond accordingly. Employees are the first and best resource. Take care of them, and they will take care of you.

2.

A FIRM'S GREATEST ASSET? RESPONSE EDUCATION

Phyllis Sorenson commented on the previous article.

I wrote back to Phyllis Sorensen, Utah Education Association

Dear Phyllis,

Thank you for responding to the January 2, 2000, newspaper article "A Firm's Greatest Asset? Workers." BYU just forwarded it to me. I am honored that you would respond and wish you well in the forthcoming 2000 Legislative Session. You have a big job ahead and a very important one.

As a preface, I might mention that I am very sympathetic and supportive of education in general and keeping our efforts focused on our main customers, the students. My father was a school teacher for almost 40 years. I love and honor the educators who taught and inspired me and appreciate so much the efforts of both teachers and administrators who do the same today for my children and others.

Currently, it appears that Utah is training a great generation of new teachers every year only to watch them leave for "greener pastures." While that may be a great blessing to the rest of the country, Utah is beginning to feel the effects of teachers who love teaching, but have to spread their time, energy, attention and interest to provide for their families. Recently, we hired two brothers to build shelves in our garage after their regular school day as teachers in two schools in Utah County. They work from 4-9 p.m. each night, 4 week nights and on Saturday so they can continue to teach school. They love to teach and they love their students, but they have known since they began that this extra work outside of school would be necessary. They make great shelves, but I told them, and they agreed, that it is ironic that we as a community are quick to critique the "system," but slow to invest in it. We can be proud and brag about our GNP and even more amazed at the trends in the stock market, but by and by we will reap the returns of our investments and commitment in education.

Phyllis, you asked me if I "have feelings and thoughts about unions in general or the Utah Teacher Association (UEA) in particular." Indeed I do, and I would love to meet you in person to learn of some of the issues, challenges and approaches you face. Undoubtedly, there are things we would be agree on 100 percent, and others we may have fun arm wrestling over. However, if I could offer any support to help you stay "on the right track," as you said, it would be to mention a few quick strategic thoughts for you and the legislature to keep in mind. They include this advice for teachers and everyone involved in schools, including the UEA:

1. Always keep focused on who your primary customers are—students!

2. Never forget that while the methods may vary, the purpose of providing educational services is to enlighten minds, build character and develop individuals.

3. Reward for performance and innovation. This applies to students and educators.

4. The marketplace will determine the products and services. We are all customers in that marketplace.

5. Follow wise political strategies.

6. Implement sound business practices.

7. Unions, like any social group, can make great contributions, as well as be responsible for terrible injustices. You will determine which. Much of the outcome will depend on the spirit you have and actions you take.

My goodness, I did not intend to wax so philosophical. Practically speaking, you have been placed in a unique and important position. Seek the best counsel you can from those with wisdom and experience. Do your best. We have a wonderful democratic process of debate and compromise. Pray as Abraham Lincoln did, not that the Lord would be on his side, but that he would be on the Lord's side.

As a citizen, I would ask that you fight for all you're worth to get good teachers the pay that will reward and incentivize them to dramatically improve student education. Fight equally hard to hire and retain the best teachers, and release those that should not be in the system. Fight to protect the opportunity to learn, but more important, preserve the desire and hunger for truth and knowledge and its appropriate application.

Again, thank you for your response. God bless you; I will pray for you and the others.

Sincerely,

Dale Christensen

3.

A NEW WAY OF THINKING

Response to September 11, 2001 Terrorist attacks on the World Trade Center in New York City, and on the Pentagon in Washington, D.C.

Government and business leaders, as well as ordinary citizens, need to put on their entrepreneurial hats when dealing with serious and complicated world problems such as the recent terrorist attacks.

More than ever before, we need to look outside the box and facilitate creativity, innovation and synergy in harmony with truth and principle in order to design and sculpt peace and prosperity in the world. The world needs entrepreneurial vision and practice at its best to find solutions to its current problems.

For the past several months I've been teaching entrepreneur and management communications to MBA students in the business school of the University of Science & Technology of China (USTC). In a great effort to reform its economic system and further open up to the world, Chinese educational institutions started offering MBA programs in 1991.

Experts estimate that in 1999, about 20,000 people were enrolled in Chinese joint venture MBA or executive MBA programs to promote excellence in entrepreneurship. They believe that China currently needs more than 300,000 MBA graduates to satisfy its development needs. Worldwide, the need is even greater.

China has experienced rapid and positive progress during the twenty years since opening up to the West. However, innovation and entrepreneurial initiative are key ingredients that need to be developed. In my entrepreneur class, I encourage students to look for new and better ways to solve problems and meet the needs of the marketplace, which are many and varied.

While I try to avoid discussing sensitive subjects, it was difficult when students asked my opinion about the destruction of their embassy in Yugoslavia. My sincere answer of deep concern for this terrible incident opened them to further questioning. You can imagine their questions following the collision between the U.S. spy plane and China's fighter.

While I knew only what they knew from the TV reports, we all agreed that this was a serious problem, amplified because the Chinese people were hearing one story and the American people were hearing another.

So what were we to do about it? I divided the class down the middle. The right side was to represent an American public relations firm advising the Chinese government on how to better communicate with the American people. The left side was a Chinese public relations firm advising the U.S. government on how to better communicate with the Chinese people. What an exciting and enlightening discussion we had that day! I wish both governments could have listened in.

Chinese people do not know or understand Americans, and we don't really know and understand the Chinese. We are all struggling to overcome "the enemy" syndrome, get acquainted, and be good neighbors. It appears that there are some who don't want us to be friends. Continued criticism and more "accidents" make it even harder.

Neither side can claim being without fault. Now, more than ever before, all nations need entrepreneurial vision and staying power to be competitive and progressive, and still be a good neighbor.

Now students are asking, "What do you think, and how do you feel about the terrorist attacks? What will the U.S. do?" Once again, we had a very energetic and almost inspiring discussion about innovative and alternative solutions to this terrible problem and some of its apparent causes.

We concluded that the government leaders of all nations need to think and be entrepreneurial as they separately or unitedly proceed. If not, they may be creating more problems for future peace and entrepreneurial opportunity.

4.

THE AMERICAN DREAM

Today, the American Dream is so many things to so many people. It has grown from a simple desire for religious freedom to an ever-increasing wish for everything you can imagine. What is your American Dream?

To some it is being able to start with nothing and become famous, wealthy or powerful. To some it is being able to choose your own profession, own your own home, and send your children to college. To a growing number, unfortunately, it is being able to live the good life at someone else's expense.

Through the decades, this dream has evolved. It began with an abiding trust in God and his blessings upon the people of this land. As the Native Americans were being driven off their lands, their dream was to fight off the invaders and preserve their way of life.

For the Pilgrims, it was religious freedom from persecution and or control by the Church of England. They risked their lives and those of their loved ones to escape the oppression that was preventing them from worshiping God according to the dictates of their own conscience. There was an awakening and a growing expectation in the hearts and minds of people in many countries who would not give up their sacred beliefs, even though it meant punishment, imprisonment or even death. Their loyalty to country and love of family and friends was overshadowed by their love of God and a yearning for self-realization and expression. These few put their trust in God, set an example, and blazed a trail to a place for others to follow.

They were followed by wealthy merchants and land barons who sent advance teams of explorers and settlers to pick the low-hanging fruit of opportunity in this new world. Some came for opportunities to earn a better living than they could do in their home country, others for adventure and curiosity. But almost all came with an abiding faith in the hand of Providence acting on their behalf as they traveled the swift currents of progress. They prayed for safety on the high seas. They prayed for strength and power to fend off and defeat the "native savages" in the new land.

Then came the starving masses, the prisoners, and the slaves to do the work of civilizing a new world. Some sought a better life while others were forced from family and home to be pressed into labor for the benefit of their masters. Most had nothing but God to turn to for hope. They prayed fervently for compassion and mercy and pressed forward to improve their lot in life in mortality or beyond.

The American Dream was encouraged and taught in homes, churches and schools. It was a new philosophy, a new way of living and becoming. Patriots pushed back against foreign efforts to control and tax. As a result of many events, this dream was memorialized in the *Declaration of Independence* and in *the Constitution of the United States.* War galvanized the colonies and blood bought and paid for the right of every citizen to dream the dream and live the life it promised.

In spite of religious revivals and exponential growth of churches and clergy, conflicts and wars, both foreign and domestic, continued to shape and define the realization of the American Dream. With love for country and fellowman, all prayed to God for victory. Men such as Abraham Lincoln advised the country to pray that they were on God's side, instead of praying for him to be on theirs. But always, there was prayer. Always, there was God.

Through many decades of constant, and sometimes necessary, opposition and conflict, Americans moved in the same direction of manifest destiny while acknowledging Divine help. However, in the United States today, many people only dream of fame, fortune and freedom, without remembering the originator of this great dream.

Without God, there is no real purpose or plan, and the dream changes to a nightmare of pride, greed, hate and lust for power. With God, the dream lives on.

What does this great and much-talked about American Dream mean to you?

5.

CONSULTANTS AND COACHES MAKE GOOD BUSINESS

Business owners often act like impulsive teenagers. They get swept up in mainstream thinking and behavior without seeking out or relying on available wisdom and experience. They follow their emotions and impulses rather than really thinking about what's going on. When allowed to do so, parents help their teenagers make and implement good choices. Business maturity would suggest that experts can help owners make good choices and implement strategies.

The greatest leaders in the world, and the most successful business people, have sought out and demanded counsel from their wisest and most-trusted advisors. Edgar A. Guest wrote, "This is wisdom, maids and men, knowing what to say and when. Speech is common, thought is rare. Wise men choose their words with care."

The usual resources available to entrepreneurs and small businesses include friends, family and business associates who can often only offer common sense and basic "business first aid." However, while they have great desires to help, these people seldom have the expertise or skill to really give advice. Members of an advisory committee or board of directors can give periodic assistance, but seldom are they affordable or available as needed.

Just as your yearly physical checkup is desirable, so is a regular business audit. Business consultants and coaches can and should be brought in occasionally for "thorough examination, diagnosis, prescription and surgery if needed." Consulting is appropriate evaluation, analysis and recommendation. Coaching is "tough love" implementation of strategies to help business owners optimize resources to get desired results.

In the professional world of sports there are owners, managers, coaches and players. Coaches play a vital roll to train, motivate, discipline, strategize, and deal with personal issues. They serve as a liaison between players and owners. The roles of coach and manager are very different. Frequently in business, top employees are promoted to be a manager and find that they are a good employee, but a poor manager.

There are coaches in many areas, such as in weight loss, music, and drama, but not in business. Why? Independent consultants can assist owners to work "on" the business, and independent coaches can work "in" the business with a team concept to help owners define the roles and realize results. These experts can provide credibility and experience to help optimize their client's resources. Such strategic consultation and coaching implementation can increase the company's productivity, revenues, and profits, as well as the owner's equity and control. At the same time, they can help decrease expenses, employee turnover, and stress so the owner can enjoy a fuller life balance and measurable business success.

Remember when you were a child and you always wanted to win the game? If you were a leader, you usually won by picking the best players for your team. Now the stakes are higher. How do you get the best players to play on your winning team? You have to either offer them part of your company, or risk big dollars on high salaries and executive packages.

Most small businesses don't have the resources to even consider building their "Dream Team" in the early years. As the company grows, they begin to think they don't need such a team.

However, successful entrepreneurs and wise business owners seek out and utilize a team of seasoned veteran consultants who already have the expertise and professionalism. They often become the MVP partner on the team. Owners realize they don't have to go it alone or give up their company to get the job done.

Look around and ask others who the best consultants and coaches are. Consultants and coaches make good business. As you grow and struggle, think about who your consultant is, and who is coaching you. Business consultants and coaches can make a big difference.

6.

STEW LEONARD'S CUSTOMER SERVICE

Last week, my wife purchased a large bag of oranges from Stew Leonard's, a local food store located off Exit 7 on Federal Road in Danbury, Connecticut. Going through the bag at home, we noticed that there were half a dozen oranges that were overripe and spoiling. We agreed that it would be only fair to return them for six good ones.

When Mary-Jo returned from her errands, she was impressed about what she had experienced at Stew Leonard's. I overheard her telling someone on the telephone what had happened. Later that night at a family birthday party, she again related the experience to our extended family, explaining that when she had asked for the exchange of the oranges, the young female clerk at the customer service desk insisted on giving her a whole bag of fresh oranges. Not six, but a whole bag!

Mary-Jo said, "That's so nice, but just a fair exchange is all I expect."

"No Ma'am, just go and get another bag," the clerk said.

So Mary-Jo left to make the exchange, and she picked up some apples and other items on the way. She ended up buying a lot more than she had planned to. Then, when she was paying at the cash register for the things in her cart, a young man came up and gave her a large bag of grapefruits with a sticker marked "Paid" over the $3.99 price tag.

He said, "I want you to take this also, in exchange for the oranges."

Surprised, she said, "You don't have to do that."

The employee replied, "Yes, please take it for your trouble."

My wife always loves to shop at that store, but you can imagine how good she felt that day. She has told the story to many of her friends. Within a few days, people in several states and even out on the West Coast had heard the story. I have also told that story many times. It was the very thing that inspired me to write this book. As a matter of fact, I'm enjoying some of that delicious fruit as I write.

You know, that was the best advertising money Stew Leonard's could have spent. That bag of oranges and the bag of grapefruit sure went a long way—a very long way. You could almost say that it has gone the extra "thousand miles."

Stew Leonard's is the store that I like to shop in almost any time. This family store has a great reputation for superior products and uncommon customer service. It is noteworthy to mention that people come from quite a distance to buy great produce and to have a unique shopping experience. It's a huge barn, shaped with a children's petting zoo of farm animals at one end of the parking lot. The parking is adequate, but most people would walk across the street if they had to. I would, too.

When you walk in the front door, you pass a Wishing Well that invites you to donate the change in your pocket to a worthy charity. Can you image? Before you get in the door, they invite you to give your money away for nothing in return. Helping others goes far beyond their store.

Then you begin to experience shopping at Stew Leonard's! You see their store rules carved in a huge two- ton stone right in the middle of the wide aisle. You can't miss it. The two rules the store lives by are:

Rule #1: The customer is always right.
Rule #2: If the customer is ever wrong, re-read rule #1.

In another location, on a large hanging sign, every customer is able to read Stew Leonard's Mission Statement:

"We work to make happy shoppers!"

Wow! What about that?

Do you think they succeed 100 percent of the time? Probably not, but they sure are close.

Immediately upon entering the large open doorway of the store, you smell the sweet aroma of freshly baked goods that is piped in just for such enjoyment. You begin to salivate, and no matter when you've last eaten, you're hungry all over again. The ice cream bar is on the one side and the popcorn treats and an assortment of flavored coffee beans on the other.

My favorites are all the free samples. As you go past the baked goods there are assorted samples of the most delicious muffins and cookies or little cups filled with samples of cherry or apple pies and plastic forks to eat it with. There may be samples of shrimp dip and shrimp at the seafood bar or ham, chicken or roast beef at the meat counter. Just enough to feel satisfied and leave you with the feeling that you want to come again.

It is fun to take visitors from out of town to Stew Leonard's just so they can share the experience. Recently I took my brother through when he came to visit while on a business trip. I said, "If I were a homeless person, I would live next door to this place and come here every day." I'm surprised that lots of other stores haven't duplicated what they are doing here.

The Leonard family started as a small dairy store with a limited number of items. They have grown much larger, but they keep that personal touch that keeps people coming back. Kids love to go there with their parents. It's like a small entertainment center. There are talking and singing chickens, cows and milk cartons that are started by pushing buttons that are easy to reach by the kids and a person dressed up like a cow just wandering around entertaining the kids both young and old. There's a whole generation growing up that will be shopping at Stew Leonard's for the rest of their lives.

Two years ago, my friend David Logie from Hartford stopped in at Stew Leonard's with his family on their way back from a weekend vacation in New York City. They had gone to see a couple of plays, the museums, and some of the tourist sites. He wanted to exchange some free ice-cream tickets someone had given him quite a while before. His whole family loved it. When they were again traveling east on I84 toward home, he asked the kids what they enjoyed most about the weekend. Almost in unison they enthusiastically responded, "Stew Leonard's!" He leaned over to me and said, "Can you imagine that? After all the planning and effort, to say nothing of the expensive hotel and other expenses that had totaled over several thousands of dollars, they liked Stew Leonard's the best, and I didn't have to spend a dime!"

Customer service is more than just providing superior products or services. It's all about how you make people feel and how they feel about you.

7.

GO! GO! CEO!

"A good adventure needs to combine some risk-taking, some unvisited, untracked, or unexplored territory, and some physical challenge."
--Dick Bass, in *The Seven Summits*

Dick Bass, the developer of the Snowbird Ski Resort near Salt Lake City, Utah, was wearing a neck brace when I first met him on a plane. Soon he was telling me of his philosophy and passion to development "body, mind and spirit." Simultaneously, he was selling me on coming up to visit his ski resort called Snowbird where "the powder snow is waist deep. There's no place in the world like the Bird. Come and ski with me!"

He told me about some of his life adventures, which included: climbing the highest mountains on each of the seven continents, including Mt. Everest; getting married on top of the Matterhorn; swimming the Dardenells two-and-a-half miles across Hellespont; and jogging the 31 miles over the original route that the ancient Greek runner Philippides ran when he carried the marathon victory message to Athens.

Dick feels that he always does his best when he has a challenge right in front of him to focus on. He has developed an optimism that gives him the ability to smile in the face of adversity and have faith that through hard work and smart work, everything will work out. He always eliminates defeatist thoughts from his mind. He quotes his uncle as having said to him after losing the election for president of the student council, "Just remember, men are made strong not by winning easy battles, but by losing hard-fought ones."

Even in defeat Dick was positive and quoted Falstaff: "He who fights and runs away, lives to fight another day, but he who in the battle is slain, will never rise to fight again." He always faced an uphill battle of convincing people in an almost evangelistic manner that he could build Snowbird and climb the mountains. He wrote, "People are always doubting my ability to be able to do what I set out to do. I'll show them. . . ."

As a CEO, we need a whole-life philosophy, implemented with systems that provide other people with everything they need to increase their productivity, find and preserve peace and happiness, and enjoy a healthy balance in life. Only then can they magnify themselves, their spheres of influence, and their organization. We must learn how to expand horizons and be more effective through learned principles, practices, and skills.

We do not have to be successful or wealthy to be happy, but we do have to give our best efforts. We must learn to achieve inner peace and balance in life and deal with unexpected demands and interruptions. Self-confidence comes by using correct principles and skills to identify our highest priorities, set and achieve meaningful goals, and reduce stress.

8.

A GUIDE TO GREATNESS

A young man once asked Socrates for wisdom. The two waded chest deep into the sea, where Socrates took him by the scruff of the neck and held his head underwater until the man was exhausted. After recovering, the young man confronted Socrates and demanded an explanation. Socrates answered, "When you want wisdom as much as you wanted air, you'll find it."

Not long ago, someone asked me how to become a great leader. Remembering Socrates, I answered, "If you really want to succeed in becoming a great leader, you'll find the way." Then I gave what I call "A Guide to Greatness."

First and foremost, found yourself on integrity and honesty in all things. Align decisions and behavior with proven principles. Seek truth and divine inspiration. Remain teachable, open-minded and willing to listen to expert advice. Guard your reputation and honor your word. Negotiate to seek fair results for all parties.

Be values driven, mission focused and passionate about what you do. Be goal oriented and self-motivated. Plan and effectively manage your time and resources. Think strategically; anticipate future moves, and adapt through alternative plans and exit strategies. Do the right things rather than just do things right.

Surround yourself with people of high caliber, and build on your combined strengths. Find the right person for the job and the right job for the person. Be relationship-governed. Network to develop alliances with trusted partners.

Strive for excellence and quality by setting measurable standards and focusing on both performance and results. Inspire people to stretch for goals beyond their expectations and focus more on quality than quantity. Don't lock into system-approaches at the expense of people and flexibility. Be a calculated risk taker and wise risk manager by understand the value of timing.

Continuously improve, learn from mistakes and make adjustments. Be creative and act outside the box. Challenge conventional practices and search for new and more effective solutions. Recognize change as an opportunity and not a problem. Become expert in monitoring, measuring and analyzing performance and progress. Focus on the 20 percent effort that gives 80 percent of the results, and take the initiative to get things done.

Be a leader and mentor who gives vision, direction, and inspiration to others. Be decisive, even at personal risk, and consider how your decisions affect others. Communicate the broad picture. Ask key questions about expectations. Invite feedback and make it safe for others to disagree.

Keep things in perspective. Be willing to compromise with others to stay on target. Being tolerant and open will help you deal effectively with those whose views and backgrounds are different from your own. Resolve conflict constructively by: 1) directly focusing on the issue, not the person; 2) helping participants to stay neutral; and 3) keeping private things private. Anticipate problems, and seek solutions.

Be service orientated and work for the benefit of the whole rather than just personal interests. Involve others in decisions. Help others understand how they contribute to the organization's mission.

Believe you can, and you will. Work toward it by being that kind of person. Leaders are successful and great for many reasons, but mainly because they have integrity and they believe and persist in doing the right things.

Great leaders choose to be optimistic, to believe, and never give up. Their success is in the achieving and enjoying what's most important. Socrates could have said it better, but I believe this is how one becomes a great leader.

9.

HORATIUS AT THE BRIDGE

From a poem by Thomas Babington Macaulay (1800-1859)

Great people seemingly cause the tide to rise, and that tide lifts all boats. This principle is dramatically described in the epic poem, "Horatius at the Bridge" by Thomas Babington Macaulay. There are moments in time when true greatness and courage shine forth for the whole world to see. Such was the case with Horatius with his two brave companions, Spurius Lartius and Herminius. Attitude, timing, and action make all the difference. The story is as follows:

Lars Persona of Clusium and his massive army of 80 thousand foot soldiers and 10 thousand horsemen were burning village after village on their way to conquer Rome. For two days and two nights they marched onward, clouds blackening the sky by day and flames lighting up the sky by night. Then a scout rode swiftly to report to the Fathers of the City that he was nearing the city just on the other side of the swollen and raging Tiber River.

The Consul could see the swarthy storm of dust rise fast along the horizon. The trumpet's war cry was heard repeatedly, and then the long lines of spears and helmets could be seen. Disheartened, the Consul admitted that they would be overrun before they could destroy the bridge across the river to stop their foe on the opposite bank. Then brave Horatius, captain of the gate, spoke up and said, "To every man upon the earth, death cometh soon or late. And how can man die better than facing fearful odds, for the ashes of our fathers and the temples of his gods? Hew down the bridge, Sir Consul, with all the speed ye may; I, with two more to help me, Will hold the foe in play. In yon strait path a thousand may well be stopped by three. Now who will stand on either hand, and keep the bridge with me?"

Without hesitation, Spurius Lartius and Herminius spoke up and stepped up to support Horatius in this overwhelming and certainly deadly challenge. The three soldiers raced to their position, tightening their armor while the Fathers, mixed with commoners, "seized hatchet, bar and crow to loosen the sturdy planks above and the strong props below." Meanwhile the enemy's ranks, like a sea of gold, surged and rolled forward toward the bridge's head. "Four hundred trumpets sounded a peal of warlike glee." All eyes were on the bridge's gate "where stood the dauntless three." They waited calm and quiet and watched the vanguard stop and listened to the loud laughter that rose throughout the ranks. Then three chiefs rushed forward, dismounted "before the mighty mass." They drew their swords, "lifted high their shields, and flew to win the narrow pass."

First, came Aunus of Tifernum, who was hurled into the river by Lartius. And then "Herminius stuck at Seius, and clove him to the teeth; At Picus brave Horatius darted one fiery thrust, and the proud Umbrian's gilded arms clashed in the bloody dust. But now no sound of laughter was heard amongst the foes. A wild and wrathful clamor from all the vanguard rose. Six spears' length from the entrance halted the mighty mass, and for a space no man came forth to win the narrow pass.

But hark! The cry is Astur: and low! The ranks divide; and the great lord of Luna comes with his stately stride. Upon his ample shoulders clangs loud the fourfold shield, and in his hands he shakes the brand which none but him can wield." With his broadsword in both hands, Astur rushed at Horatius and "smote with all his might."

With his sword and shield, Horatius was able to turn the blow, but the blade came down and "gashed his thigh." A cry went up at the sight of blood. He reeled and momentarily rested on Herminius and then "like a wild cat made mad with wounds, sprang right at Astur's face. Through teeth and skull and helmet so fierce a thrust he sped, the good sword stood a handbreadth out behind the Tuscan's head."

With a heel on his throat, Horatius pulled out his sword. The Roman crowds on the distant banks cried for the three to return before the bridge fell. "Spurius Lartius and rminius darted back; and, as they passed, beneath their feet they felt the timers crack." Safely across they turned to see brave Horatius standing alone at the gate. They started back across, "but, with crash like thunder, fell every loosened beam, and, like a dam, the mighty wreck lay right athwart the stream." A long shout of triumph and relief rose from all the walls of Rome, but no one could help Horatius, who stood alone against the massive foe.

"Down with him!" cried false Sextus, with a smile upon his pale face; "Now yield thee," cried Lars Persona, "Now yield thee to our grace!" Then Horatius slowly turned around without responding and looked to the white porch of his home, "O Tiber! Father Tiber! To whom the Romans pray. A Roman's life, a Roman's arms, take thou in charge this day!"

"So he spake, and, speaking, sheathed the good sword by his side, and with his harness on his back, plunged headlong in the tide. No sound of joy or sorrow was heard from either bank, but friends and foes in dumb surprise" watched as he sank and rose. With blood flowing and "heavy with armor, and spent with changing blows," he struggled on and finally felt his feet on solid ground. In victory, he was carried out and above the joyous crowd with shouts and clapping and weeping loud.

10.

MADE IN AMERICA

As a young boy growing up in the 1950's, I remember getting small, cheap toys labeled "Made in Japan." The first food I saw with that label was "chocolate covered ants." I wasn't very impressed with those things.

My pride in "Made in USA" grew as the years went by, knowing that people all over the world wanted what we had. Then Japanese products began to compete. They were attractive. Their reputation improved and became the standard. All of a sudden they were front and center, manufacturing methods dominated, and "Made in Japan" had a whole new meaning. They became equals along with the German, Swiss, and Belgium names. American manufacturing and marketing were forced to retool and redirect. The competition began! For the next three or four decades, the players were looking at any way to win.

Meanwhile, Dung Xiao Ping, a small leader in the big country of China, opened China's doors to the West and entered the race. His motto and reason for change was, "It doesn't matter if the cat is black or white, as long as it catches the mouse." With an abundance of cheap labor and an appetite for manufacturing and western culture, China began to attract and take in foreign jobs.

The sucking sound was beginning to be heard in every nation in the contest. More and cheaper parts and products were wanted by consumers all over the world. This demand could only be met by what China could bring to the table, and everyone wanted to partake. New trade organizations were formed, and treaties were drafted to open the way for the free flow of goods to consumer's homes and offices. The frenzy was sweeping in everyone, everywhere.

Both multi-national and domestic companies scrambled to give contracts to produce everything. A few concerned economic philosophers predicted the massive loss of jobs and unemployment to Americans.

Now we are finding the cost too high. Millions of manufacturing jobs have been exported to Asia, and the economic results are now unfolding. The United States walked out of the industrial age and into the information age, but we gave our means for strength and success to Asia. What can be done? Will "Made in America" be remembered only as a label, or can it be regained as a way of life?

11.

OLYMPIC MEDALS: AN ENTREPRENEURIAL ADVENTURE

The Salt Lake City 2002 Olympics was one of the best lesson in entrepreneurship the world could have asked for. The Olympic motto, "Stronger, Higher, Faster" is also the driving force for almost every new business venture. It is being seen and felt more and more by people all over the world. To just know that it is possible is enough to inspire the mind and heart to new and better possibilities.

The Olympic athletes see the vision, they dream the dream, and then they relentlessly and courageously pursue their goals. Most of them risk everything they have, including their safety, to not only win the gold medal, but to compete as an Olympic athlete in the world games. They invest their time, energy, money and future in an effort to achieve their goals.

When planning a career and looking for that first job after graduation, it seems wiser and safer to go with the "sure thing" like a national or multi-national company. With these jobs, there if usually security, a steady paycheck, and prestige, etc. Others have already blazed the trails and built the bridges to these "lands of opportunity." Why not do this instead of taking the risk on your own to start something new? The graduate has studied and earned the right to harvest these benefits.

Perhaps there's no such thing as a sure thing. What if you'd chosen to go with Enron, Ernst, K-Mart, or some other giant who fell by the sharp economic sword or competition's piercing arrows of the marketplace?

America was founded on the spirit of entrepreneurship. It was created by people willing to risk their honor and wealth and even their lives to achieve something new and better for themselves, and especially for their posterity. There are always some who perpetuate that spirit. Why not be one of them?

12.

PERSONAL PLEDGE

How many times have we thought, or heard someone else say, the following: "Politics is a nasty business. I don't want any part of it. I don't want to put my family through that mess." Or they say, "I'm not going to waste my time to vote because one vote doesn't make any difference." Or, "All politicians are crooks, and I won't vote for any of them."

Do we realize that these are the thoughts and attitudes that allow bullies and tyrants to gain power and dominance? These kinds of attitudes are giving away our God-given rights protected by the U.S. Constitution. If we want to maintain freedom, we have to work and fight for it. If we are not willing to work and fight, we deserve what we get.

Time and time again great men and women of this blessed land have risen to the occasion in order to fight for defend God, family and country. The price of liberty has cost the blood of each generation. The conflict is always the same; the struggle is manifest in a multitude of conflicts, and victory is always temporary.

When faced with the daunting task of preserving their dreams of freedom, the Founding Fathers stepped up pledged their lives, fortunes and sacred honor. Together they faced the grave possibilities of dishonor, financial ruin and death if they did not succeed.

There are always individuals and powers trying to control the destiny of others while the common people struggle to control their own destiny. Tyrants around the world have tried to conquer and deny agency to others.

Some conflicts have been clear, while others have been confused by impure policy, practice or philosophy. Understanding of the purpose of government has diminished, while demands and expectations of government have increased. Citizens have repeatedly been spoiled, not by defeat, but by prosperity, pride and apathy. Over the past 200 years, the tides of liberty continued to ebb and flow until we now find the very life blood of our nation spilling into the sewers of waste and wantonness.

Once again, we the people of this great nation face the challenge of preserving our freedoms. We need to reacquaint ourselves with the tried and true principles of the U.S. Constitution. We need to step up and make the necessary sacrifices.

There is a call to action—a call to support the Constitution and those who defend it. We must search for honest, wise, and good men and women to represent us. We must run for office if necessary. We must make a personal pledge of our life, our honor, and our fortune. This is a call to go through the tough times, make the sacrifices, and put our families through whatever it takes to preserve our nation under God, with liberty and justice for all. This is a call to be a defender, a patriot who is willing to give and not just take. We can do it. We must do it. Will we do it? That is the question!

13.

PRISON REFORM

Every election year we hear the same arguments over and over again. There are too many taxes and too much government involvement. Or, we hear that we need more services and the government can provide them. One of the traditional issues discussed concerns our safety. This translates into law enforcement issues, including prison reform.

Does Crime Pay?

The crime rate is rising, and we have to ask ourselves, "Does crime pay?" For generations, we have heard "Crime doesn't pay." But, it appears that many people believe crime *does* pay. The crime rate is increasing, and our prisons are overcrowded. It costs the taxpayers about $35,000 per year for each convict.

Who Pays for Crime?

In the end, who really pays for the criminal's wrongdoing? The victims always pay! Yes, and if the criminal is caught and convicted, the criminal also pays in time, but the taxpayer is the one who really pays for crime.

Consumers and taxpayers ultimately pay for the expense of all preventive measures and security systems. We also pay the salaries of our law enforcement officers who arrest lawbreakers and bring them to justice. We pay for the lawyers in the District Attorney's Office who prosecute the criminals. We pay for the judges, the juries and the personnel who try and administer the cases.

If conviction is the result, taxpayers pay for months and years to incarcerate and maintain the convicts. They must be housed, fed and clothed. There is tremendous expense in rehabilitation as convicts serve their time. Serving time! That's a real oxymoron. They are serving time, but whom are they serving? They are not serving anybody! They aren't serving time; they are simply spending their time in prison. We hope they will be rehabilitated in the process. Military personnel serve time. Public servants serve time, but convicts are spending their time at the taxpayer's expense. Actually, they are the ones that are being served. In fact, all the citizens who are not in prison are serving them.

Inmate's Rights

Occasionally, we hear arguments about inmate's rights, including family visits, conjugal visits, comfortable surroundings including television, balanced meals, training and education, etc. It's easier and quicker for inmates to get these basic services than for many unemployed men and women to get unemployment payments, or for unemployed people to get health benefits. The system takes care of inmates better than it serves many homeless or needy people. Sometimes the justice of it all seems to be upside down. Sometimes the reward and punishment in life seems to be a bit confusing.

Prevention Instead of Retention

One creative entrepreneur suggested contracting with foreign governments to maintain convicted criminals in foreign penitentiaries. Very secure facilities could be built, and convicts could be fed and clothed at about 20 percent of the cost we now pay. For example, upon conviction, convicts could be immediately transported to a Chinese prison and put to use in remedial labor functions or in more sophisticated projects based on their background.

Perhaps criminals would think twice if they knew they would be sent to a Chinese prison. Escape for non-Asians would be very difficult, as they would stick out in a crowd in China. The American public would pay for these Chinese services upon the successful return of the convicts at the conclusion of their sentences.

Prison guards could be rotated frequently to prevent inappropriate relationships from developing. They could be monitored by cameras in the United States and by a very few U.S. personnel who could also rotate frequently. They would just verify that the convicts were where they were supposed to be, but the Chinese would be responsible for their security.

Truth or Consequences

If someone commits a crime, they should pay for it. They should be where they can work off their time and not just spend their time and be served by the public.

14.

QUICK CALORIES FOR BUSINESS —POWER MOVES

Experienced bikers and mountain climbers use their power bars and energy drinks for that needed boost. Likewise, entrepreneurs utilize their power resources to navigate through challenges and succeed. Such resources include: factoring, equipment leasing and outsourcing.

Factoring is the purchasing of commercial invoices or accounts receivable. It is one of the oldest and more traditional forms of business financing. One reason for business failure is inadequate cash flow because payments are often not received until 30, 60, or 90 days after invoicing.

A factoring company purchases approved commercial accounts receivable at the time goods are shipped or service is completed. They provide credit checks on existing and potential customers to help reduce credit risks. 70-80% of that invoice value is paid within 24-48 hours of the time the invoices are delivered to the factoring company. The remaining amount, less their fee, is paid when the invoice is paid. There are no loans to repay and no bankers to satisfy.

Factoring offers increased profit potential for growth-oriented companies. With the cash flow problem solved, the business can focus on sales and production. Factoring helps companies to fund sales, reduce debt, improve vendor relations, and meet other financial requirements. While bridging the gap between billing and collections, this enables a business to match cash flow to cash needs.

The business can expand, retain equity, and purchase inventory. It can increase advertising, take advantage of cash discounts on supplies, avoid additional debt, and be free of restrictions imposed by term loans or conventional lines of credit. Factoring is not a loan; it is a purchase of invoices that costs between 3-8% of invoice amount, depending on length of time needed.

Equipment leasing is a fast, easy, affordable power move. The advantage of paying cash to buy equipment is outweighed by the disadvantage that once spent, cash is not easily or quickly recovered. The balanced use of debt and equity will produce the most substantial productivity, profits, and market gains. Leasing of an asset can replace the need for expending precious cash when alternative financing is available. Now, more than ever before, all types of equipment are leased.

There are direct leases, operating leases, finance leases, leverage leases, sale and leasebacks, just to name a few. Leasing is flexible financing that can be customized to your company's needs while offering structured rents, renewal and purchase options, upgrades to equipment, and 100% financing of equipment costs.

Leasing preserves bank credit lines. You "lock-in" your costs, thereby avoiding the very real effects of inflation and variable interest rates found in conventional financing. You can enjoy a more rapid write-off because the lease term is shorter than the depreciable life of the equipment. Retaining operating capital by leasing allows full employment of that capital. Other means of financing require significant down payments. Lease payments can be tailored to match your cash flow needs even if the business is seasonal. Payments can be timed for the use of the equipment, when it generates earnings. Projections are simple because payments are known and fixed.

More than 80 percent of American businesses lease their equipment. Leasing is an intelligent capital equipment acquisition alternative for businesses.

Outsourcing is becoming one of the most common business power moves these days. Companies outsource everything from personnel, manufacturing, fulfillment, and customer service.

There are many wonderful resources available to entrepreneurs and business managers to help them succeed. So just be prepared, utilize these power resources as needed, and good luck!

15.

SMELLL THE FLOWERS

When was the last time you heard your spouse or a friend say, "Don't forget to smell the flowers along the way." Perhaps you need to take inventory and evaluate the things that matter most. This can mean different things to different people. Regardless, there are some common denominators for most of us.

Many young entrepreneurs say, "When I become financially independent I'm going to give back to society, contribute to good causes, help the less fortunate, and travel, while spending lots of time with my family."

A few follow through and do remarkable and praiseworthy things. Others haven't quite got it yet, but still have good intentions. Too many, however, are just chasing rainbows and thinking that someday they'll get to it. To those of us in this latter category, what we have never seems to be enough; not enough money, not enough things, not enough time or energy. Forgotten are the idealistic dreams that originally inspired us to risk and sacrifice our today for a better tomorrow.

When we lose sight of our purpose of life, we are not fulfilled when we do reach or surpass our goals. We just end up with stuff that's measured in power, fame or fortune. If our purpose is neglected along the way, we are empty handed indeed. Some find themselves without family or friends and are emotionally bankrupt. We see so many of the wealthiest people living unhappy and unfulfilled lives. Is it possible that they lost their way or forgot what the journey was all about? Did they miss the best part of the journey, smelling the flowers for themselves while planting seeds for others?

There are many wonderful people who continually focus their efforts for good purposes. They leave their comfort zones and give to help the less fortunate. We will call them "social entrepreneurs." They are teaching, financing, and building. Their goal is to help others help themselves and have a better life.

We are reminded that wealth is relevant. All of us are rich in the eyes of most other nations. Each of us can do something right now to help others. Remember the quote, "I am only one, but I am one. I can't do everything, but I can do something. That which I can do I will do, and it will make all the difference."

Think and act now. Think of being financially independent right now. Be a philanthropist right now. It doesn't matter how much we're worth or the size of our income. Some may think it's heresy to have motives other than financial profits. They may feel that financial success or winning at any cost is the American way. They're wrong, and will find themselves alone. They may win the contest, but what is their prize?

In sports we can do our best, play by the rules, and be good sports. Sadly, some athletes are losing this vision. In business we can be the best and still be honest and help others, even our competitors. Remember the old movies, *It's a Wonderful Life*? We choose whether to be a happy Mr. George Bailey or a miserable Mr. Potter.

So when someone says, "Smell the flowers," take inventory and do something good! Include a bit of social entrepreneurship in your business plan and in your immediate life's goals. Reach out to someone. You will feel wonderful, and you will be a better entrepreneur.

16.

THRILL SEEKERS IN MODERN TIMES

What an entrepreneur does in his or her spare time impacts the whole company. In his article "Why CEOs Seek Thrills," Gerhard Gschwandtner discusses why "some people swim with sharks, go skydiving or bungee-jumping, or set a world record in a hot-air balloon. . . . Those who seek thrills are good for business. When a business idea takes root in the mind of an entrepreneur, it is hard to tell if the person owns the idea or the idea owns the person."

Sandra Gurvis outlines the profile of entrepreneurs in her article, "Thrill Seekers." She describes their "desire for variety, novelty and change. They're independent thinkers who are always looking for new angles. They're self-confident and have a high level of energy. Generally they are also people who started with nothing, or at most very little, and rose to the top."

Ian MacMillan, a professor at Wharton, believes that many successful business leaders begin their thrilling journey to success with what he calls "entrepreneurial insight." MacMillan goes on: "While thrill seekers get an adrenaline rush from courting physical danger, success seekers in business can experience the same excitement while launching a new business. Eager to turn their idea into reality, entrepreneurs are willing to embrace uncertainty and laugh at the possibility of loss. While they generally learn from other people's mistakes and experiences . . . they also fail. For them, failure is a benchmark to be expected and learned from."

However, successful entrepreneurs know how to plan and reduce risks. They are always "looking for loopholes and windows of opportunity which show them exactly what they need to do or the way to go. Today, the world is complex. Competition and challenges are constantly changing. It's like being in the wild. . . . What resources do you need in order to survive? They thrive on unpredictability and in situations where it's hard to anticipate an outcome," says Dr. Frank Farley. "They are looking at the future instead of the past, anticipating the next adventure. If not undertaking a new business quest, thrill seekers may be tackling a different sport or artistic avocation."

Most forms of human creativity do involve risk. Dr. Farley suggests that the risk is not always physical. "Successful innovators feel the need to go beyond the status quo, to let go of the handrails of life-traditions, customs, and the usual way of behaving in order to accomplish an inner vision."

Richard Branson, CEO of Virgin Atlantic Airlines, once said, "Being an adventurer and an entrepreneur are similar. You're willing to go where most people won't dare." Branson, who risked his life trying to circle the globe in a hot-air balloon, believes that risk taking is not about thrill seeking. It's about not wasting one's life. Earlier, he wrote, "I wanted to go on a grand adventure, to do what a lot of people dream about, but actually never get around to."

This is actually the source of the "charm" of these adventurous people because they are more interested in motivation and challenge than in management or setting strategy. Everything is a test and an adventure. However, Dr. Zuckerman warns that entrepreneurs need to maintain control and balance. He says, "It's more than just skydiving or mountain climbing. . . . Sensation seekers express themselves in many ways, including seeking new experiences or searching for stimulation through travel, arts, and crime or in overindulgence in alcohol, drugs and sex."

Sandra Gurvis concludes her article by pointing out that "Everyone has a personal mountain to climb. By tackling what seems most intimidating, anyone can mine inner strengths that lead to ever-greater peaks of success." Indeed, entrepreneurs who are climbing mountains in their spare time affect the whole company and everyone associated with it.

17.

WAR OF WORDS— A MEDIA REVOLUTION

The First Amendment guarantees that no laws will be established that will infringe on an individual's freedom of speech. The original intent was to protect citizens from fear of intimidation or reprisal if the citizens felt the need to criticize government policy.

Through the years, this protection has been high-jacked by different kinds of despots. They use it to protect perverted forms of expression like pornography, but refuse to permit it to protect expressions of prayer in public schools or exhibit Judeo-Christian values such as exhibiting the Ten Commandments in a courtroom.

Media moguls inundate the media with biased and exaggerated stories in order to quench the public thirst for sensational drama, vice, and violence. The cultural war is being fought and won on TV and over the airwaves. Most people are disturbed by this and keep asking, "Why?" The country is wondering what is happening to our schools, our public police force, our military and our government. The world is watching America on TV and only seeing a decadent, immoral and spoiled society.

The media moguls would have us believe that our youth is a lost generation. Ninety-eight percent of their focus is on a few troubled teens who hurt others and capture public attention as they cry out in their pain. The other two percent of media focus is on the good service and achievement of the vast majority who are preparing to lead this country in the future and trying to solve the many problems we will leave them.

The media moguls would have us believe that all citizens, including police and public officials, are borderline criminals, and that vice and violence is the norm. Where is the media coverage on the multitude of compassionate and helpful efforts of family, neighbors, and workers? Are reporters now too lazy to work for good reporting? Is it too easy to just chase the sirens and ambulances?

By focusing on a few, our government officials are portrayed as a bunch of greedy, immoral, power hungry carpetbaggers. Media moguls would have us believe that there isn't a city, state or national elected public servant who wouldn't rob their own mother, abandon their family, and commit treasonous acts. The media is destroying all confidence in the government, suggesting that none of them can be trusted. Only the media can be trusted. After all, we have the "First Amendment."

Media moguls, beware of the thousands of good reporters, editors and related media experts who love truth and justice. They are the soldiers who will fight the new media revolution to overthrow you. They will right the wrongs and bring stability out of the chaos you are creating. They will turn the focus on you, and the world will watch your own downfall and demise.

These truthful media soldiers have the choice of helping you take freedom from the people and bring the country into anarchy while you hide behind the First Amendment, or they will expose you for what you are and what you are doing. The Great Wizard of Media Oz must stop manipulating public opinion. It must bring the United States back to reality and protect freedom of speech as it was intended.

Let it be known that you are the tyrants to be feared the most. Your pens and cameras are mightier than the sword, but not mightier than truth, goodness and reason. You are an enemy to be feared. The struggle will be long and hard, but goodness and reason will prevail.

18.

WHY NOT A HYBRID?

Part of the definitions of the word "hybrid," according to Webster's dictionary, are:

> *"3. anything derived from heterogeneous sources, or composed of elements of different or incongruous kinds; a composite formed or composed of heterogeneous elements."*

Some of the characteristics of hybrids include: bigger, stronger, disease resistant, new, best of both, and out of the box.

There are advantages and disadvantages to hybrids and non-hybrids. Usually the advantages outweigh the disadvantages. For example, hybrid wheat and soy beans are preferred for their many nutritional and high-yield qualities. Cross breeding cattle dominate the pastures and stockyards across the world. The mule, a cross between a horse and a donkey, is admired for its size, strength, intelligence and personality.

In today's world, "hybrid" denotes an automobile that gets great gas mileage, conserves fuel, and is partially battery-driven. It's simple, and it's a great idea. It's a result of innovative thinking. It benefits mankind and the environment. But, if it's such a great idea, why aren't more people driving a hybrid? Why doesn't every government agency have a fleet of hybrids instead of traditional vehicles? If fossil fuel is so expensive and pollution so bad, why doesn't the government give bigger incentives to buy a hybrid?

We've been hearing about hybrid cars for many years. We've been hearing about global warming, pollution, and the high cost of fossil fuel for years. We've been hearing about difficult political and economic problems stemming from fossil fuel sourcing.

How was it that during World War II, resources were mobilized and allocated to get a job done quickly? Weapons, aircraft and vehicles were invented, adopted, and produced to meet the war effort needs. Well, we're at war, and we have war effort needs, but things seem to be lumbering along at a less than impressive rate. Could it be that the powers that be are managing this transition to benefit the large auto makers and oil companies?

If it's time, why not let the oil industry go, not gracefully or slowly, but go now! Let's get to it and make it happen. This means everyone needs to be involved and change their thinking. This means we all need to be driving hybrids. Why not hybrid vehicles, using hybrid fuels, driven by hybrid people with hybrid thinking?

Part IV

Sermons Delivered

1.

INTRODUCTION: WHAT I BELIEVE

I am a son of God, who is my Eternal Father. He is a glorified being who loves me and has given me the opportunity to become like him. I believe Jesus Christ was chosen in our pre-earth life to be our Savior and example. In our pre-earth life we followed him in the great conflict with Lucifer and those who followed him.

Christ came to earth to suffer and die as part of his atonement for our sins, and to be resurrected. I believe the Holy Spirit, or the Holy Ghost, is a personage of spirit teaches and influences us in many ways.

Adam and Eve were the first of God's children to come to earth. They were given two commandments—to multiply and replenish the earth, and not to partake of the fruit of the tree of knowledge of good and evil. By partaking of the fruit, they would bring sin and death into the world. They couldn't keep both of these commandments. They broke the one commandment in order to give all of God's other children the opportunity to have bodies and be tested. Adam and Eve were responsible for their sins, and every other person will be held accountable for their own.

Through the atonement of Jesus Christ, everyone can be saved from sin and death by accepting him as their savior and by obeying the laws and ordinances of his Gospel. The first principles of the Gospel are faith and repentance. Faith is acting on our beliefs to accept truth. Repentance is feeling sorry for our sins, stopping our evil behavior, doing good, and accepting Christ.

I believe in paying diligent heed to the words of Jesus Christ, who will bring us unto God the Father.

> *"And I now give unto you a commandment to beware concerning yourselves, to give diligent heed to the words of eternal life. For you shall live by every word that proceedeth forth from the mouth of God. For the word of the Lord is truth, and whatsoever is truth is light, and whatsoever is light is Spirit, even the Spirit of Jesus Christ. And the Spirit giveth light to every man that cometh into the world; and the Spirit enlighteneth every man through the world, that hearkeneth to the voice of the Spirit. And every one that hearkeneth to the voice of the Spirit cometh unto God, even the Father"* (D&C 84:43-47).

The first ordinances of the Gospel are baptism by immersion for the remission of sins and receiving the Gift of the Holy Ghost. Both must be administered by a worthy man who has the priesthood authority to do so.

God calls his servants by prophecy and by the laying on of hands by those who are in authority to do his will and to build his kingdom here on earth. I believe his kingdom includes The Church of Jesus Christ of Latter-day Saints, which has the same organization that existed in the church in Jerusalem during Christ's mortal ministry. This church has the same officers and manifestations of the same gifts of the spirit as existed anciently.

I believe the Bible is the word of God as far as it is translated correctly. The Book of Mormon, the Doctrine and Covenants, and the Pearl of Great Price are also the word of God. They are all testaments of Jesus Christ and are supported by living prophets and apostles who are also seers and revelators. God has revealed many wonderful things through his ancient and modern prophets, and he will reveal many more great and important things in the future. We are preparing for the Second Coming of the Messiah.

I am of the lineage of Ephraim, son of Joseph who was sold into Egypt by his brothers. All of Israel is being gathered, including the restoration of the ten lost tribes of Israel. Zion will be called the New Jerusalem and it will be built here upon the American continent. Jesus Christ will reign personally on the earth for a thousand years of the millennium. Then the earth will be renewed and glorified.

I believe I have an inalienable right to worship God according to my own conscience. In doing so, I respect the rights of others to do the same. I look to the government for protection, and I recognize my responsibility to obey and sustain the laws of the land. It is my responsibility to be honest, virtuous, praiseworthy, and to serve others with love. I look for the good in people and strive to make the world a better place.

General Observations

Every person has agency to choose between good and evil. All people are also responsible for the consequences of their decisions and actions. Every person on the earth has the light of Christ to help them discern between good and evil. The Holy Spirit can also guide people to truth. True freedom comes from using our agency to choose obedience. Loss of freedom comes from disobedience. We should repent when we sin or make mistakes. We will be blessed if we keep the commandments and follow the Holy Spirit.

Our family and friends are gifts from God and should be honored and treated with great respect. We should dress modestly and use clean and uplifting language. As we are patient, forgiving, and serve others, we will develop love for them. We should treat all people with respect and dignity.

We should seek out all that is good and uplifting and reject anything that degrades. We should be grateful for our body and nourish, exercise, and rest it appropriately.

The Fullness of the Gospel

I believe that as a member of The Church of Jesus of Latter-day Saints, we enjoy the fullness of the Gospel of Jesus Christ through living prophets and the Spirit of revelation. Through the restored scriptures, I am able to understand our pre-earth life and the purpose of our present earth life. I feel blessed to also catch occasional glimpses of the future and our post-mortal life. There are many blessings in store for us personally and for our families who will be there with us.

In conclusion, there is much I know and believe. There is also much I do not know. Amid life's many challenges, we often find it difficult to see life clearly, but someday all will be in full view and clear focus. The Apostle Paul expressed this so well when he said, "For now we see through a glass darkly; but then face to face: now I know in part; but then shall I know even as also I am known."

2.

ABYSSINIAN & OTHER BAPTIST CHURCHES

One Sunday (June 30, 2013), my wife and I visited the Abyssinian Baptist Church on 138th Street in Harlem, where we were serving a church mission. It was an inspiring service. The chapel seated four or five hundred people. A few days later, we invited one of the other missionary couples to attend the Wednesday night program by the Total Praise Ensemble in concert. Both Sunday and evening services were packed with church members and tourists.

We got there early to get a seat. They have an hour prayer, singing, and testimony service before the main program. They had microphones in all the isles, so when there was a silent moment, I stood and bore testimony. I first explained that we had attended services on Sunday and were inspired by Pastor Butts' sermon about Jesus Christ and tithing. I echoed his words that I, too, "am not ashamed of the Gospel of Jesus Christ." I heard some "Amens" and a few "Hallelujahs."

I testified of the things we had in common. God lives. He is our father and we are all brothers and sisters. Jesus is the Christ and the Savior of all mankind. I went on to testify of the principle of tithing and mentioned the Lord's promise in Malachi. The smiles, raised hands, and applause indicated that my testimony was well received.

In Harlem, where a large part of the population is African American, I am reminded that because of the great evil of slavery, the whole nation suffered in a horrific Civil War. Many wicked people suffered or were destroyed, along with many innocent people. It is always like this with tyranny.

War on Poverty

Some Americans of African descent have risen above this to realize the American Dream. However, many still languish in hatred, indolence and self-pity. Notice, I don't say, "Languish in poverty." Poverty is not imposed. It may be promoted by government programs, and it may be accepted and become a person's own bondage, but it is not imposed for the long-term, as many would have us believe.

No war on poverty will eradicate poverty. Only building individuals will do that. This must be done by love and with light and truth, not by law.

Dr. Martin Luther King, Jr., rejected, ". . . adding deeper darkness to a night already devoid of stars . . . Hate cannot drive out hate: only love can do that."

Government programs and free lunches will only keep people alive. They can't give people freedom. I believe that God works from the inside out. The world works from the outside in. The world tries to take the people out of the slums. God takes the slums out of people, and then they take themselves out of the slums. The world tries to mold men by changing their environment, but God changes human nature. Changed people can change the world.

Lead Us Out!

In the Old Testament, the Children of Israel needed Moses. Americans of African descent needed Frederick Douglas, Abraham Lincoln, and Dr. Martin Luther King, Jr. But where are the leaders of today? Where are leaders speaking the truth and warning people of the real bondage and slavery?

People need to be warned to avoid the bondage of personal and national debt. This is slavery offered by the Welfare State and accepted by individuals and families that results in self-imposed limitations. None of us can afford to stay in this Egypt of bondage any longer.

Free at Last

There is also slavery of hate and pride, envy, immorality and evil. There are those who want to keep the fires of racism and hatred burning so people cannot let go and love their neighbor. There are those who want you to be puffed up in your pride so you will not have an open mind and heart to accept light and truth. They would also have you envy and covet so you will steal from others.

They want you to support government and programs designed to legalize the taking from those who have and give to those who have not. Your church can do this as a community service and you can willingly do this as an individual. But, to have someone forcibly take from you and give to others for purposes that you do not believe in or support, is not the purpose of government. The purpose of government is to protect against such practices.

There are evil powers, individuals, and organizations that want you to speak vulgarities and to watch pornography. They do not appeal to our highest and best, but to our lowest and basest. They want you experiment with immoral acts of any kind so it won't seem bad to lie, cheat and commit fornication and adultery. There are always promises of wealth, power and fame or popularity. They want to have you force others to do wicked things or destroy them if they refuse. This is slavery and imprisonment.

A person who is addicted to drugs, alcohol, tobacco or any substance or evil behavior is a prisoner and a slave. A victim can suffer injustice, humiliation or bullying and still be free. However, the perpetrator of the injustice is truly a slave and prisoner.

Dark Horse Candidate Running

You can say that you heard today that I am running for President of the United States. What are the qualifications for the office of President? The President must be born in the United States and have lived in the U.S. for at least fourteen years. The President must be at least thirty-five years old. The President's powers are limited to serving as Commander in Chief of the Army and Navy; nominating advisors, officers, and judges; making treaties; giving pardons; and signing into law the bills passed by the House of Representatives and the Senate.

The president has an obligation to be a leader and try to persuade citizens and governmental officials to act according to just laws and to encourage them to change unjust laws. However, this leadership must not be abusive or dictatorial. The President must swear an oath to defend the U.S. Constitution.

I vow to be this kind of a president. I vow to follow the Constitution and the guidelines it sets forth for the President of this great country. I vow to be dedicated to the principles that will be in the best welfare of the people, no matter where their original family roots began. We are all here now, and must be unified in morality and clarification of purpose.

I Love New York

Harlem

I love New York and especially living in Harlem, I felt it was my full-time job to say hello to everyone and smile at them.

Wishing others a good day lifted my spirits at the same time. I always tried to be prepared with some quarters, dimes, nickels or pennies to give to beggars on the street. Occasionally, I had to keep some back to give to another on the next corner. Maybe it didn't help them much, but it helped me a lot.

Are You Obedient?

My favorite greeting to younger children was to ask if they obeyed their parents. I talked to many hundreds of children. They would usually look to Mom and Dad for approval to answer. I had the parents' ear and even the attention of many others on the bus, train or sidewalk. Then I would say, "If you obey your mother (or father), you will always be happy. That's my promise! If you don't obey, I can't promise you happiness." The children usually nodded their head affirmatively or began telling me what a good boy or girl they were. The parents almost always gave me a smile a big silent, "Thank you!" as we moved along.

Be Good and Be Great

With older children and teenagers with backpacks, sports gear or even I-phones, I'd ask if they were a good student or good at what it looked like they were going to do. I mostly got, "Yeah, I'm good or pretty good." Then I'd say, "Don't just be good, be great! You can be great. The difference is in how you think and how you feel in your heart."

At the end of the day and at the beginning of each day I have an opportunity to dust away negative thoughts from my mind and wash away the bad things in my heart. I'm grateful to be alive! I'm glad to be able to make a difference. I'm happy I can be great and help others be great too!

3.

ADVERSITY

Adversity Is Part of Life

We understand that in order to progress, it is necessary to experience opposition (2 Nephi 2:11). We also understand that men have their own agency to choose the good from the evil in all things.

Personal Peace

In temple recommend interviews this past year, I have made a special point to challenge each church member to try to live what I have called the "Spirit of the Word of Wisdom." It is true that we can enter the temple if we don't use tobacco, alcohol, coffee, tea, or abusive drugs. However, if the Gospel really does include all truth, and if that truth will make us free, there must be more.

My suggestion to each person in the interview has been to eat properly, get the right amount of rest for your age and activity, be active and exercise regularly, and finally, be happy. Most people accept this as common sense and good health as well as being a commandment of God. In D&C 88:124-126, the Lord outlines several keys to good health and stress fitness.

Occasionally, a faithful church member will ask, "Why am I not happy? I attend church and pay my tithing. I try to keep all the commandments the best I can, but I just feel terrible." We might well ask ourselves, when we feel like this, if we are keeping the "letter" of the commandments or the "spirit" of the commandments. We may be going through the motions of being a disciple of Christ, but we might be spiritually asleep, ill, or even dead. (2 Cor. 3:6) We feel like the salt that has lost its savor (Matt. 5:13).

While the Lord has been generous in giving us guidance to achieve personal peace, we must seek and find, ask and receive, knock and enter (Matt. 7:7). We will not be commanded in all things (D&C 58:26), and we recognize the necessity of opposition (2 Ne. 2:11). So we can have at least some consolation in knowing that we are all going through a natural process called "mortality."

In today's world, we are bombarded by so many opportunities, demands, pressures and responsibilities. The Gospel of Jesus Christ is the answer to coping with it all. He has given us the "hidden treasures of knowledge" (D&C 89:19). It is very possible that being humble or patient may dramatically affect health and longevity as much as not smoking or drinking alcohol. Perhaps these *principles* may have a more dramatic effect than those *practices*. As we consider these possibilities, let us not look beyond the mark of their prophetic purpose in relation to our eternal salvation. Their spiritual significance comes first, but the physical effects are both interesting and important.

What might be some of the *physical* results of good *spiritual* hygiene? Here are a few principles Christ taught; let's see how they affect our stress level or sense of peace:

1. Prayer – preventive, focused, direction;
2. Ponder – quiet meditation is a healthy, reflective practice to help us hear God speak to us; and
3. Forgive – there is nothing more therapeutic or healthy than to forgive and let all the negative energy of our body, mind and soul leave us to grow and flourish.

In an issue of *Prevention* magazine, I came across a special report titled "Pray for Peace - How to Enhance the Relaxation

Response through the Faith Factor." Dr. Herbert Benson, M.D., then professor of medicine at Harvard Medical School and president of Harvard's Mind/Body Medical Institute, was quoted regarding the "relaxation response," a physiological response characterized by decreased heart rate and blood pressure and feelings of tranquility. He teaches patients to "sit quietly in a comfortable position, and silently repeat a word or phrase." He said, "My study in this field has convinced me that, for whatever reason, faith does make a difference in enhancing the power of the mind over health and disease . . . in all different religious contexts, there seems to be a similar potential for health-enhancing effects."

He suggests that we "choose a word or a short phrase from your religion. Repeat the word or phrase silently to yourself, coordinating it with your breath if that's most comfortable. The words should be easy to pronounce and remember, and short enough to say silently as you exhale. When thoughts arise, as they inevitably will, gently return to the focus word. You'll begin enjoying periods of stillness and quiet in your mind." In the same article, Dr. Joan Borysenko, Ph.D., notes that "Meditation is defined in all spiritual traditions as a kind of focusing."

While walking around the high school track with my wife, I thought that Henry Marsh, Olympic athlete and stress fitness expert, should write an article for the Ensign to help Latter-day Saints and others to understand the close relationship of physical stress-related diseases and our observance of the basic principles of the Gospel. With quotes by renounced athletes, physicians, scientists, philosophers and General Authorities perhaps it would help many to develop "divine behaviors" for reasons other than blind obedience.

Accentuate the Positive

Christ taught action, not passivity, when he said: "He that believeth on me, the works that I do shall he do also; and greater works than these shall he do" (John 14:12); and . . . "Be ye doers of the word, and not hearers only" (James 1:22); and also, "I would that ye wert cold or hot. So then because thou art lukewarm, and neither cold nor hot, I will spue thee out of my mouth" (Revs. 3:15).

Knowledge and belief are passive. Knowledge or belief plus action becomes faith. Faith is active. We exercise faith. We do works by faith. "All things are possible to him that believeth," but it's only when we act that these things come to pass. Almost all that Christ taught requires action. He taught us to have faith, repent, be baptized, receive the Holy Ghost, pray, thrust in our sickle, preach, sacrifice, love, give, go, do, have patience, lose our life in service, and endure to the end.

You don't think these require action? Christ also taught that now is the time for action. Today! This moment, this life. Alma taught, "For behold, this life is the time for men to prepare to meet God; yea, behold the day of this life is the day for men to perform their labors" (Alma 34:32).

Eliminate the Negative

> *"And if thy right eye offend thee, pluck it out, and cast it from thee: for it is profitable for thee that one of thy members perish, and not that thy whole body should be cast into hell"* (Matt. 5:29).

When necessary, be strong enough to shut off the television or get rid of it altogether. Now that's a revolutionary idea. One that will not be very popular. I have suggested this to some of my Latter-day Saint friends who are having serious problems at home. I get the same response from them that I get from people who don't want to give up tobacco or alcohol. They argue moderation in all things. That was my favorite argument.

One good sister made the comment to me that "Without the television her family wouldn't know what to do. It was broken for a week and it was like one of the members of the family was gone." I know the feeling. Like many of you, I am a reforming TV addict. I'm convinced that I would be fine if I had six TV sets all going at once. A basketball game on one, a football game on another, two good movies going on sets three and four, and a news broadcast on five, with some good entertainment on number six. I'd be just fine, but my wife can't get through to me when there is just one set on, let alone six. Besides that, my home teaching never got completely done, and I seldom frequented the temple.

My wife and I were married for four years before we got our first television set, and within the first year, I could see that she wasn't happy. The practice of watching the six o'clock news straight through until eleven just wasn't her idea of family life. I gave our TV to my brother, and now his wife complains and says she wishes I hadn't done it. I should write a book called *Life after TVS*.

Leaders, when you see discouragement or apathy creeping into the lives of those you serve, it may be because they are spiritually ill or dying because of neglect or sin. They may be just falling asleep due to inactivity. I have heard the statement by some that, "I became inactive because I was overworked" or "I got burnt out from too much work." This shouldn't happen if we are serving with the right spirit and purpose. It may be because things are out of balance or out of control, but great blessings are promised to those who go the extra mile. The Lord won't ask us to carry more than we are able to bear. He promised us that his burden is light.

4.

AFFIRMATIONS IN SHARING THE GOSPEL

These thoughts and words will help us act and react in a more powerful manner. We can express our gifts, talents and desires in a powerful way. We do great things by acting accordingly. The following are some examples:

Personal Affirmations

- I have faith in God and in myself.
- I am honest and accept myself.
- I know who I am, and I know my strengths and positive qualities.
- I am no better than anyone else, and no one is better than me.
- I accept compliments well.
- My mind is naturally goal seeking.
- I am becoming what I think about.
- I feel good about what I know, and I believe in what I do.
- I am happy and at peace with myself.
- I have an indomitable spirit and a positive attitude.
- I change my life by changing my attitude.
- I identify needed change, give myself orders to make the change, and follow these orders.
- I have character. I carry out my worthy decisions after the emotion of making that decision has passed.

Action Affirmations

- I serve others.
- I don't run faster than I am able.

- I am a successful person, and I am willing to do what others are not willing to do.
- I deal in specifics, and I succeed.
- I have specific goals and a burning desire to achieve them.
- I measure and record my performance, and my increasing performance accelerates.
- I am in good physical shape, and I condition my body regularly.
- I look good and dress to succeed and to feel good.
- I am fluent in my body language and know what my body is saying.
- I read good literature, observe uplifting things, and avoid pornography and bad literature.
- I listen to and observe great speakers and examples.
- I learn from others who have succeeded after many failures.
- I sacrifice good things for better things.
- I control my time and the events in my life.
- I don't let rejection slow me down.
- I work hard and never give up.

Affirmations Regarding Others

- I have charity toward all people.
- I accept others as they are, regardless of how they act, and I use their hostility to my advantage.
- I look others in the eye.
- I smile and sincerely compliment others.
- I treat others as they ought to be not, as they are.
- I associate with good people.
- I belong to good organizations.

Affirmations of Missionary Skills

- I know the Gospel and know the Gospel is true.
- I learn all I can before teaching.

- I am worthy and teach by the Spirit.
- I know the requirements of baptism, and I am accurate and positive about them.
- I know the emotions and reasons that cause people to listen and accept.
- I see everyone as a potential investigator.
- I know that each person has specific desires and needs.
- I know that each person wants to know how I know truth.
- I listen and ask questions to discover each person's desires and needs.
- I qualify every person and keep an accurate and neat referral file.
- I proselyte (using all methods) to keep my pipeline full.
- I capture the person's attention and make smooth transitions to Gospel discussions.
- I am specific when calling to make appointments.
- I create the proper setting and spirit.
- I do not fear failure.
- I avoid early dismissal and never apologize for taking a person's time.
- I remove tension as soon as possible.
- I am a friend, not an adversary.
- I control the interview or discussion.
- I demonstrate the Gospel through living it.
- I read body language and understand that timing is critical.
- I recognize acceptance signals and a desire to know more.
- I explain the things I teach by scriptural reference.
- I recognize objections as a request for more information and handle them immediately.
- I never argue and deal with the real problem.
- I know my success ratios.
- I am committed and commit others.

5.

ANGELS FROM ON HIGH

We Are Not Alone

Angels exist and are empowered by Jesus Christ through His infinite Atonement.

> *"Have miracles ceased? Behold I say unto you, Nay; neither have angels ceased to minister unto the children of men. . . . It is by faith that miracles are wrought; and it is by faith that angels appear and minister unto men; wherefore, if these things have ceased wo be unto the children of men, for it is because of unbelief, and all is vain."* Moroni 7:29 & 37

Angels have ministered to or communicated with Adam, Hagar (see Genesis 16:7–11), Manoah's wife (see Judges 13:3, 6, 19–21), Daniel, Mary the mother of Jesus (see Luke 1:26–38), Mary Magdalene, Salome, Joanna, Mary the mother of James, other women (see Mark 16:4–6; Luke 24:2–4; John 20:11–12), Peter, Paul, John the Revelator, and many others. Angels have also ministered to Book of Mormon characters, including Nephi (see 1 Nephi 11:14; 2 Nephi 4:24), King Benjamin (see Mosiah 3:2), Alma the Younger (see Mosiah 27:10–11; Alma 8:14), Amulek (see Alma 10:7), Samuel the Lamanite (see Helaman 13:7), and others.

Furthermore, in our own dispensation prophets and apostles have testified of the eminence and considerable standing of angels. In fact, our dispensation has been a period of extraordinary angelic activity. Joseph Smith received dozens of communications from angels. Additional Church authorities and others have been recipients of angelic communications.

The Church of Jesus Christ of Latter-day Saints was restored, in part, when angels imparted revelations and truths to the Prophet Joseph Smith. A passage in the Doctrine and Covenants summarizes: The voice of Michael, the archangel; the voice of Gabriel, and of Raphael, and of divers angels, from Michael or Adam down to the present time, all declaring their dispensation, their rights, their keys, their honors, their majesty and glory, and the power of their priesthood. (D&C 128:21)

It is appropriate to speak about angels. Elder Jeffrey R. Holland wrote, "I believe we need to speak of and believe in an bear testimony of the ministry of angels more than we sometimes do.

"In the gospel of Jesus Christ we have help from both sides of the veil. When disappointment and discouragement strike—and the will—we need to remember that if our eyes could be opened, we would see horses and chariots of fire as far as the eye can see, riding at great speed to come to our protection. They will always be there, these armies of heaven, in defense of Abraham's seed."

There are *hosts* of angels. Hosts means "angelic armies of heaven." The term *Lord of hosts* sometimes refers to "the heavenly beings" or "a large number of people or things." The plural, *hosts,* multiplies this number. The Lord of hosts of angels refers to immense numbers or "an innumerable company of angels." (Revelation 5:11)

Indeed, ten thousand times ten thousand angels, which equals 100 million, symbolizes a great number. To sum up, there are numberless concourses of angels, an innumerable company of angels, and hosts of angels—all of whom are in the service of our Lord and God.

Angels Protect the Righteous

Angels are agents of power and are formidable beings. They can power to protect us from harm and danger and serve as a reassuring force. Their power ultimately exists because of Jesus Christ and His Atonement.

Daniel in the lions' den was protected by angels. A stone was placed over the den's opening to prevent Daniel's escape. Then, to ensure that possible coconspirators with Daniel would not remove the stone without detection, the king and his officers used their signets to seal the stone (Daniel 6:17). Had the seals been broken during the night, the king and his officers could have claimed deception or trickery on the part of Daniel. But neither the rock nor the seals prevented the angel from entering the den and stopping the lions' mouths. We note that the angel was not only empowered to save Daniel but that the angel himself was also immune from the lions' destruction. Because of Daniel's faith and righteousness, the angel saved him from a horrific death. Daniel would later testify, "My God hath sent his angel, and hath shut the lions' mouths, that they have not hurt me: forasmuch as before him innocency was found in me" (Daniel 6:22).

During the reign of **King Hezekiah the Assyrian** army was advancing toward Jerusalem with the intent of conquering it. With scores of thousands of enemy soldiers camped outside of Jerusalem's gates, waiting to destroy the city's inhabitants, Hezekiah petitioned the Lord through prayer in the temple. In response to Hezekiah's humble prayer, the Lord sent his prophet Isaiah to the king, promising deliverance from the Assyrian army. Soon thereafter "the angel of the Lord went forth, and smote in the camp of the Assyrians a hundred and fourscore and five thousand" (Isaiah 37:36; see also Isaiah 37:33–35; 2 Chronicles 32:21). It is sometimes difficult to comprehend such extraordinary dominance: one angel versus some 185,000 disciplined soldiers—and the angel was victorious. Such an angelic operation is permitted only according to the Lord's divine will.

When **President Harold B. Lee** was serving as the president of the Church, he shared an experience that occurred while he and his wife were traveling on an airplane. They had been visiting a mission, and both were impressed to return home earlier than they had planned. As President and Sister Lee were sitting in the airplane, homeward bound, President Lee received a blessing from an unseen person. He related:

> *As we approached a certain point en route, someone laid his hand upon my head. I looked up; I could see no one. That happened again before we arrived home, again with the same experience. Who it was, by what means or what medium, I may never know, except I knew that I was receiving a blessing that I came a few hours later to know I needed most desperately . . . Shortly* [after we arrived home], *there came massive hemorrhages which, had they occurred while we were in flight, I wouldn't be here today talking about it. I know that there are powers divine that reach out when all other help is not available . . . Yes, I know that there are such powers.*

The **attempt of Syria's king to capture Elisha**. During the night the king surrounded Dothan with soldiers, horses, and chariots. When Elisha's assistant awakened early in the morning, he saw the armies that surrounded the city and cried out to Elisha, "Alas, my master! How shall we do?" Elisha replied by saying: "Fear not: for they that be with us are more than they that be with them." After this reply, Elisha prayed, and said, "Lord, I pray thee, open his eyes, that he may see." And the Lord opened the eyes of the young man; and he saw: and, behold, the mountain was full of horses and chariots of fire round about Elisha. (2 Kings 6:15–17)

President Henry B. Eyring said, "I know that the promise of angels to bear us up is real. You might want to bring to memory the assurance of Elisha to his frightened servant. That assurance is ours when we feel close to being overwhelmed in our service. Elisha faced real and terrible opposition. . . . Like that servant of Elisha, there are more with you than those you can see opposed to you. Some who are with you will be invisible to your mortal eyes."

Elijah and Elisha were walking and talking near the Jordan River, and "there appeared a chariot of fire, and horses of fire, and parted them both asunder; and Elijah went up by a whirlwind into heaven." When Elisha witnessed this scene, he cried out, "My father, my father, the chariot of Israel, and the horsemen thereof" (2 Kings 2:11–12). On April 3, 1836, this same Elijah visited Joseph Smith and Oliver Cowdery in the Kirtland Temple. Joseph wrote, "Another great and glorious vision burst upon us; for Elijah the prophet, who was taken to heaven without tasting death, stood before us" (D&C 110:13). Earlier, an angel provided food and water to the prophet Elijah when he fled for his life from Jezebel (see 1 Kings 19:1–7).

Some individuals who attended the **dedication of the Kirtland Temple** beheld angels, horses of fire, and chariots to protect the Saints from Satan's host of evil spirits. The Prophet Joseph Smith recorded: "The heavens were opened unto Elder Sylvester Smith, and he, leaping up, exclaimed: 'The horsemen of Israel and the chariots thereof.'" Joseph Smith wrote that Elder Roger Orton saw a mighty angel riding upon a horse of fire, with a flaming sword in his hand, followed by five others, encircle the house [temple], and protect the Saints, even the Lord's anointed, from the power of Satan and a host of evil spirits, which were striving to disturb the Saints.

Joseph Smith envisioned Elder Brigham Young standing in a strange land, in the far south and west, in a desert place, upon a rock in the midst of about a dozen men . . . who appeared hostile. He was preaching to them in their own tongue, and the angel of God standing above his head, with a drawn sword in his hand, protecting him, but he did not see it.

Angels in This Dispensation

Angelic communications are not reserved for those who lived during the ancient periods, nor only for prophets, apostles, or notable women. Indeed, several of our Church authorities have clearly taught that we who are lay persons may receive angelic communications according to the divine will of our loving Heavenly Father.

President Boyd K. Packer, "Angels attend the rank and file of the Church. . . . Who would dare to say that angels do not now attend the rank and file of the Church who—answer the calls to the mission fields, teach the classes, pay their tithes and offerings, seek for the records of their forebears, work in the temples, raise their children in faith, and have brought this work through 150 years? Angels attend the Church's rank and file as they raise children in faith, pay tithing, conduct sacred temple work, teach classes, and more. The operations and ministrations of angels are largely unknown to mortals. Angels can move about the earth conducting the Lord's divine work, and they serve, minister, and mingle among mortals, usually without our awareness. Most of us in mortality will never see an angel."

Parley P. Pratt said that angels can "be present without being visible to mortals."

Paul wrote, "Be not forgetful to entertain strangers: for thereby some have entertained angels unawares" (Hebrews 13:2).

Elder Dallin H. Oaks taught how angels may communicate to us who are mortals, including you and me. "The ministering of angels can also be unseen. Angelic messages can be delivered by a voice or merely by thoughts or feelings communicated to the mind . . . Nephi described three manifestations of the ministering of angels when he reminded his rebellious brothers that (1) they had 'seen an angel,' (2) they had 'heard his voice from time to time,' and (3) also that an angel had 'spoken unto [them] in a still small voice' though they were 'past feeling' and 'could not feel his words' (1 Ne. 17:45). . . . Most angelic communications are felt or heard rather than seen. Unseen angels communicate across the veil to mortals by thoughts or by feelings. It is by faith that angels appear and minister unto men" (Moroni 7:37).

Elder Heber C. Kimball related an occasion when he and Brigham Young traveled together, conducting the Lord's work. They started out with only $13.50, but along the way they paid for a number of items, including travel, lodging, and meals. In fact, they paid out over $87.00, although they had only had $13.50. Elder Kimball stated, "Brother Brigham often suspected that I put the money in his trunk or clothes, thinking I had . . . money which I had not acquainted him with, but this was not so. The money could only have been put in his trunk by some heavenly messenger who administered to our necessities daily, as he knew we needed."

Angels are Agents of Love

All angels minister with heavenly love, and every angelic communication to the Saints is a message of love. Oliver Cowdery personally witnessed the love of John the Baptist when John appeared to him and Joseph Smith. Oliver wrote that this angel's "love enkindled upon our souls."

President Joseph F. Smith spoke during general conference in April 1916 of the love of heavenly messengers: "I believe we move and have our being in the presence of heavenly messengers and of heavenly beings. We are not separate from them . . . I claim that we live in their presence, they see us, they are solicitous for our welfare, they love us now more than ever . . . Their love for us and their desire for our well-being must be greater than that which we feel for ourselves."

Parley P. Pratt remained captive for months in a Missouri dungeon. He was very discouraged. After fasting and praying for a number of days, he experienced a powerful answer to his prayer. He wrote: "A personage . . . stood before me with a smile of compassion in every look, and pity mingled with the tenderest love and sympathy in every expression of the countenance . . . A well-known voice saluted me, which I readily recognized as that of the wife of my youth, who had for near two years been sweetly sleeping where . . . the weary are at rest." This personage, as an angelic messenger, delivered her message to Elder Pratt and then departed.

President Brigham Young spoke on the subject of female angels: "Suppose that a female angel were to come into your house and you had the privilege of seeing her, how would she be dressed? . . . She would be neat and nice, her countenance full of glory, brilliant, bright, and perfectly beautiful, and in every act her gracefulness would charm the heart of every beholder. There is nothing needless about her."

President Ezra Taft Benson, who recounted an eternal love story of his wife's parents. His father-in-law, Carl Christian Amussen, a convert from Denmark, was a watchmaker and jeweler in Utah. He passed away in 1902, leaving his wife, Barbara, a widow for forty years. In 1942 the deceased Carl came to his wife to inform her of her approaching death. What a great blessing it was for her to see her eternal companion for the first time in so many years. Carl appeared to Barbara and informed her that she would pass away on the following Thursday. Barbara had no doubt that her husband had appeared to her, nor did she doubt that she only had less than a week to live; in fact, she began to make concrete plans for her death. On Sunday at church she bore her testimony and bid the ward members good-bye. During the coming days she withdrew her savings from the bank, ordered her casket from a local mortuary, paid her bills, and even had the power and water turned off at her home. Then she went to her daughter Mabel's home to await her passing. President Benson concluded, "On the day of her passing, Mabel came into the room where her mother was reclining on the bed. Her mother said, 'Mabel, I feel a little bit drowsy. I feel I will go to sleep. Do not disturb me if I sleep until the eventide.' Those were her last words, and she peacefully passed away."

Testing Angels

There are three kinds of angels:

1. Righteous angels with resurrected bodies of flesh and bones;
2. Righteous spirits; and
3. Evil spirits.

You may test an angel to know whether they be from God or from the devil by offering them your hand and request that they shake hands with you. "If he be an angel he will do so, and you will feel his hand. If he be the spirit of a just man made perfect he will come in his glory; for that is the only way he can appear–Ask him to shake hands with you but he will not move, because it is contrary to the order of heaven for a just man to deceive; but he will still deliver his message. If it be the devil as an angel of light, when you ask him to shake hands he will offer you his hand, and you will not feel anything; you may therefore detect him. These are three grand keys whereby you may know whether any administration is from God." (D&C 129:5-9)

6.

THE BOOK OF MORMON

Read It and Share It

It is sometimes easier to study other books *about* the Book of Mormon, with all the interesting geographical theories, than to hear those ancient prophets call us to repentance. It is easier to read books about the ancient pyramids found in the Americas than to feel the Spirit of God burn in our hearts and acknowledge that we must humble ourselves and heed those promptings. It is easier to talk about the importance of sharing the Book of Mormon than to actually follow through in properly placing a copy in somebody's hands. It is even harder to challenge and commit them to read it and to pray to God to know if it is true.

As a boy just about to begin fifth grade, I had my first memorable missionary experience with a non-member. It was during a hot summer day when I met my Catholic friend, Terry Hernandez, on the curb in front of Mr. Jones' house next door. He stopped and we talked, and soon our discussion drifted to religion. He told me many things about the Catholic religion and his own beliefs. Then I told him many things about the Church of Jesus Christ of Latter-day Saints, the Book of Mormon, and the Prophet Joseph Smith. We asked each other questions, and I think we both left feeling like we had just had a very profound experience. We felt good about the exchange. However, my friend could not be coaxed to read the Book of Mormon, nor accept what I had to share.

It was earlier that same spring that I had been sitting with my family in the old Blackfoot Tabernacle while attending the morning session of stake conference. The sun shined through the big windows as the speaker preached to the congregation. It was Elder Legrand Richards, who emphatically challenged us to read the Book of Mormon and share it with the world. He had helped me take the first step.

The first convert baptism I witnessed came as a result of giving a copy of the Book of Mormon to my friend, Kevin Rank, who was also a senior at Central High School in London, England. During that year we enjoyed many wonderful activities together, including traveling all over Europe to participate in various athletic events and special school outings. It was an experience of a lifetime for me.

For graduation, I gave a copy of the Book of Mormon to all my friends. Inside the cover of Kevin's copy, I wrote something very simple and signed my name. That summer, I went to Holland to work so I could earn money for my return trip to the United States and to attend college at BYU. Kevin went to Arabia for a year to work.

During that year, away from his family's influence, Kevin read the Book of Mormon and gained a spiritual witness of its truthfulness. When he returned to the United States, he came to visit me the following summer he wanted to be baptized. Although his parents did not approve, we fasted and prayed that their hearts would be changed. One afternoon, while under the influence of the Holy Ghost, I wrote a special letter to his parents, explaining the circumstances and pleading for their approval. The following week he received a letter giving their permission.

I was privileged to perform the baptism. As we came out of the water and sat on the steps of the baptismal font in the basement of that same Blackfoot Tabernacle, we wept in each other's arms and rejoiced in the Spirit of the Lord. I'm so grateful for the Book of Mormon and for having shared it.

During my senior year, while studying at Boston College in Massachusetts, I was called on a stake mission. In the stake conference, just before he was called as a general authority, our Stake President, L. Tom Perry, gave us a challenge to have a "Month of Perfection." I recorded the following in my personal diary:

> *"During stake conference, President L. Tom Perry gave all members a challenge to have a month of perfection in our lives and repeat it often. He outlined a plan for us to choose various areas to perfect, and for thirty days be perfect in those areas (i.e. paying perfect tithing, getting up at a given time each morning, reading the scriptures for a certain amount of time each day, etc.) He promised great blessings as the result of obeying his instructions. I chose the areas I wanted to be perfect in and promised the Lord I'd be faithful.*
>
> *"As I implemented the principles outlined in the 'Month of Perfection,' I found the unfolding of the blessings that has been promised for being obedient to this challenge. Almost immediately, during the first week, there were several people who asked me about my religious beliefs, and others continued in their interest and desire to study and investigate the church. Some invited themselves to church, or asked me if it were possible for them to attend church with me."*

I shared the Book of Mormon with everyone who would listen. The first convert baptism during this stake mission was Mary-Jo Nanna, who later became my wife. I can truly testify

"How great shall be your joy with (him or her) in the kingdom of our Father!"

The prophet at the time, Ezra Taft Benson, challenged us to use the Book of Mormon in our studies and our teachings, and to place a copy with each family. Once, we took Elder Loren C. Dunn's advice and as a mission, we completely read the Book of Mormon in one month. I tried to use it in all my talks. It is the truth, and it testifies of itself. I know it is the word of God, and I know that it is a great missionary tool. Missionaries can share it with everyone. Copies of the Book of Mormon can be placed with individuals at the door, or handed to them during a discussion.

My first missionary companion only showed the Book of Mormon to someone when he felt inspired to do so. We placed on book a week, or one every two weeks, and taught very little. Having only a few months in the mission, I assumed that this was the correct way. Then, one cold winter day in Vermont, during a work visit with another junior companion, my eyes were opened. In that one afternoon we placed seven copies, and several people called us back to teach them.

Later, while speaking to the missionaries in our mission, Elder Boyd K. Packer gave a promise. He said that if we could increase the number of copies of the Book of Mormon we placed, our baptisms would increase accordingly. My companion and I decided to put his promise to the test. We hadn't had baptisms for three months. We began to place eleven a week, then twenty-one and soon thirty-three. Then, finally, in one week another companion placed sixty-six! It was a miracle, and this was in New England!

I remember very clearly the night I lay in my bed thinking, "If they can place sixty-six copies a week, then we can place 100!" Faith and desire filled my soul to increase convert baptisms.

The next day we outlined our plan and set our goal to place 100 copies in one week. To make a long story short, we met our goal in the first three days, and by the end of the week we had placed 201 copies. The next week we taught discussions continuously, and by the end of the next three months we had baptized 17 converts. Elder Packer's promise was fulfilled.

Years later, I told this story to some missionaries in Vermont who hadn't placed books or baptized for months. Just months later, when I met one of the elders in Boston, he told me they had placed 500 in one week using this technique outside a shopping mall.

When my wife and I arrived in Peru to serve as mission president, some felt that the people were too poor to pay for the Book of Mormon. It was my observation that most people could afford a bottle of beer. In my mind, I thought if they could afford that, then they could afford to purchase the Book of Mormon. I told my assistants the same experience that had happened in New England years earlier. I told it in greater detail of course, and showed them how to do it. Once we were passing through a small jungle town, and without getting out of the jeep, we sold four copies of the Book of Mormon. Then we got out and had a street meeting and sold a few more books. The elders were so excited they couldn't wait to try it on their own.

A few weeks later, in a near-by town, the assistants sold sixty copies of the Book of Mormon in one afternoon in the Plaza de Armas. They felt bad because there were twenty more people who wanted to buy a copy, but there weren't any more. The missionaries taught discussions the rest of the day. That night, as they walked home through the same plaza, they saw someone on every park bench either reading the Book of Mormon or a pamphlet.

One month shortly thereafter, the zone of Villa Maria in Lima, Peru, had a goal to place 1,000 books and baptize 200 people as a result. They only placed 500, but after the first six months they had almost 75 members the branch.

7.

CALLING OF A PROPHET

Each prophet in Biblical times received their calls through revelation from God. It was the same in the Book of Mormon times, and is the same today. Here are two examples of how a prophet is prepared or called:

George Albert Smith

In the small southern Utah town of St. George, the future-prophet George Albert Smith had a vivid dream in which his grandfather, George A. Smith, appeared to him. The setting was in a beautiful forest near a placid lake. At first, George Albert was alone and felt that he had finished his "work in mortality and had gone home." Soon he found a clearing and a pool of water with a bundle of clean clothes. He washed and put on the clean clothes and went on to find a fine house. He knocked and was greeted by his grandfather, George A. Smith. his grandfather said his grandson George was late. "Yes," explained young George, "but I am clean." The grandfather then asked what George had done with his name. The reply was that he had done nothing to tarnish it.

Heber J. Grant

President Grant was born just nine days before his father died. Jedidiah M. Grant had been a faithful apostle and member of the First Presidency of the Church of Jesus Christ of Latter-day Saints.

Heber Grant was known for the principle of self-improvement and for the church's welfare program. At the age of twenty-four he felt deep depression about not having been called on a mission, even though the patriarch had blessed him that he would be called in his youth. One day while walking on Main Street in Salt Lake City, he stopped and turned around and spoke out loud, although no one was there to hear him. He said, "Mr. Devil, shut up. I don't care if every patriarch in the church has made a mistake in a blessing, and told a lie. I believe with all my heart and soul that the Gospel is true, and I will not allow my faith to be upset because of a mistake of a patriarch." Within a few weeks Grant was called to be a stake president; he was the youngest in the entire church. In a special blessing he was told that he would one day preside over the church. He never spoke of this until after he became President of the church.

Another time, as Grant and brother George Teasdale entered the Tabernacle for General Conference, Brother Teasdale's face lighted up and he extended his hand and said, "Brother Grant, you and I are going to . . . ," and then he commenced to cough and could speak. No other words passed, but the meaning was not lost. It came to President Grant that the two of them were "going to fill the vacancies in the Quorum of the Twelve Apostles." However, no names were presented for the general body of the church to vote on. Eight days later, Grant was called into the office of the First Presidency and saw Brother Teasdale there. He knew why, because the Spirit had confirmed the reason.

Still, there was an intermittent negative spirit whispering to Grant that he was unworthy to be an apostle and that he ought to resign. When he would bear testimony that Jesus is the Christ, the Son of the living God, the Redeemer of mankind, there would often come the insidious whispering, "You lie. You lie. You have never seen him."

Later, while on the Navajo desert, Grant told his companions to go ahead. He wanted to be alone. In his own words, he wrote:

"I seemed to see, and I seemed to hear, one of the most real things in all my life. I seemed to hear the words that were spoken. I listened to the discussion with a great deal of interest. The First Presidency and the Quorum of the Twelve Apostles had not been able to agree on two men to fill the vacancies in the Quorum of the Twelve. There had been a vacancy for two years, and a vacancy of two men for one year, and the conference had adjourned without the vacancies being filled.

"In this council the Savior was present, my father was there, and the Prophet Joseph Smith was there. They discussed the question that a mistake had been made in not filling those two vacancies, and that in all probability it would be another six months before the Quorum would be complete. And they discussed as to whom they wanted to occupy those positions, and decided that the way to remedy the mistake that had been made in not filling these vacancies was to send a revelation. It was given to me that the Prophet Joseph Smith and my father mentioned me and requested that I be called to that position.

"I sat there and wept for joy. It was given to me that I had done nothing to entitle me to that exalted position, except that I had lived a clean, sweet life. It was given to me that because of my father's having practically sacrificed his life in what was known as the great reformation, so to speak, of the people in early days, having been practically a martyr, that the Prophet Joseph and my father desired me to have that position, and it was because of their faithful labors that I was called, and not because of anything I had done of myself, or any great thing that I had accomplished. It was also given to me that that was all these men, the Prophet and my father, could do for me. From that day it depended upon me and upon me alone as to whether I made a success. . . ."

8.

CHANGE AND CHAINS

People Want Change

People want change, but too often they expect others to bring it about for them. However, people also fear change. They are afraid that others may bring about change that is uncomfortable or difficult. They fear change because *real* change is a personal thing. Change is difficult because we are bound by chains of fear and doubt.

Chains of fear restrict our mobility, growth, and happiness. Samuel Johnson wisely shared, "The chains of habit are too small to be felt until they are too strong to be broken." (From the *International Dictionary of Thought)*

I invite you to be committed to change. Be committed to good and healthy living. Do the right thing. Righteous living is a shield, a protector, an insulation, a strength, and a power. Yes, living a life of righteousness is a chain breaker. You can break the chains that bind you down. You can change and progress.

Procrastination

"But I can change at any time! I think I will—tomorrow!"
Anonymous

Wake up and listen. Don't procrastinate, but believe and move forward to seek the straight and narrow course. Procrastination is a silly thing. It will only bring us sorrow. Shaking off restrictive chains requires action. These chains cannot be wished away. A declaration alone will not break chains. It requires commitment, self-discipline, and work. It requires action.

At times you might feel confused and sense a loss of spirit. Feeling totally helpless, you feel dependent and desperate. Just move forward one step at a time. Move forward in patience and commitment.

Chains of Addiction

There are many forms of addiction. Drug abusers are prisoners in their own bodies and minds.

There are also chains of murmuring and criticism. It's damaging to habitually find fault and malign someone's character or share malicious rumors! Gossip and caustic comments often create chains of contention. These chains may appear to be very small, but they can cause great misery. There are chains of arrogance and domination or making compulsory demands of others. Chains of lust and self-deceit or other damaging chains cause misdirection, family destruction, loss of self-respect and sadness. They are broken only by people of courage and commitment who are willing to struggle and weather the pain in order to change.

It is true some people do not want to change, even though they may say they do. You can only supply the motivation. The church, the home, the family, friends, and those professionally trained can aid, support, encourage, empathize, and guide, but the work of change belongs to the person. Most often, it is plain hard work.

To change or break some of our chains even in a small way means to give up some behavior or habits that have been very important to us in the past. Generally this is frightening. Change involves risks. We fear how people will react and respond to us if we change, even if our present way of life is painful and self-destructive. We sometimes think it serves a purpose, and so we become comfortable with it.

Progress Requires Risk

Every worthy change means risk—the risk of trading an old and damaging habit for a new and improved way of life. William Shakespeare said in *Measure for Measure*, "Our doubts are traitors, and make us lose the good we oft might win by fearing to attempt." (Act 1, Scene 4)

Even the chains of fear can be broken by those who will humbly seek God's help and strength. The joys of happiness can only be realized by living lofty principles.

Commitment

Those who are committed to improvement break chains by having the courage to try. Those who live without commitment mistakenly think it is easier to adapt their life-styles to the weight and restrictions of chains rather than to put forth the effort to change.

We must rely on a power greater than ourselves. This is the first step in Alcoholics Anonymous. With God's help, the chains that bind us can be shaken off by faith, works, prayer, constant commitment, and self-discipline. We can have the will and strength to shake off the chains that would control and destroy our progress,

We can also make some changes in our family culture, our ethnic culture, or our national culture if necessary for our happiness. We can be virtuous and live a chaste life. We can care for our bodies and minds and put into them only things that are good and healthy. We can be honest with ourselves and others. It is our individual choice and responsibility.

9.

DON'T BE A DARE DEVIL

Act within the Bounds the Lord Has Set

My family and I and some friends were all preparing for our annual Mount Timpanogas climb in early September. Some of the young people had become avid rock climbers. I joined my son Sam and his friend Andy to watch a movie of climbers doing some "dare devil" kinds of things. One walked a 50-foot tightrope from one peak to the next. Another climber scaled a high cliff, with very few cracks in it, without using any ropes. I was shocked and disturbed to see this reckless action, but also troubled at how these two twenty-six-year-old returned missionaries were mesmerized by what they were watching.

I love mountain climbing. My father was one of the first men recorded to climb the Teton's in Wyoming. I loved Dick Bass' book, *The Seven Summits,* describing him as the first to climb all of the highest mountains on the seven continents. His success, however, was not without hardship, danger and death.

MESSAGE:

Satan can tempt us and deceive us to do things we should not do. This can apply to our hobbies, entertainment, investments and work. Today, for the thrill of it, we see people parachuting out of airplanes and jumping off bridges while tied to a bungee cord, for the sensation of the "free fall." It is difficult for us to imagine the Savior acting like this. His teachings do not recommend such behavior.

We live in an age of unlimited abilities and unbounded limits. However, there is a difference to being inspired by the Holy Ghost to move out of our comfort zones and stepping outside of "the bounds the Lord has set." When we do that, the Spirit leaves us, and we are alone to make decisions and act. Too often, and too easy, we allow our appetites and passions to control us rather than us controlling them. Many are becoming addicted to thrills. Sometimes, tragedy and sadness are among the consequences. Then people quickly realize how foolish and dangerous some acts can be, but it may be too late for others.

Don't be a dare devil. Act within the bounds the Lord has set. Perhaps this thought may save your life.

10.

FASTING:
THE SPIRIT OF THE FAST

Gandhi

Recently, I had the privilege of going with my wife to see the movie *Gandhi.* Knowing a little about his life, I decided to go fasting so that I might be more enlightened by the story. It was very moving and has changed my life for the better. I wept when I saw the starving people in exile, those being discriminated against or beaten and slaughtered. But the overpowering message was that this one, small man lived and practiced the principle of fasting, and as a result, affected the lives of millions of people, including my own. He started strikes, he helped win India's independence, and even stopped wars by observing the fast and by marching forward. He was described as being passive, but he wasn't passive at all. He was active, always on the offense. He wasn't perfect, nor did he do everything just right, but he was aggressive in a very unique way.

Fasting has a way of putting things in perspective. It's a special help God has given us to be happy. It puts us on a higher, spiritual, more in-tune level.

Isaiah 58:6-11:

6 "Is not this the fast that I have chosen? to loose the bands of wickedness, to undo the heavy burdens, and to let the oppressed go free, and that ye break every yoke?

7 Is it not to deal thy bread to the hungry, and that thou bring the poor that are cast out to thy house? When thou seest the naked, that thou cover him; and that thou hide not thyself from thine own flesh?

8 Then shall thy light break forth as the morning, and thine health shall spring forth speedily: and thy righteousness shall go before thee; the glory of the LORD *shall be thy rearward.*

9 Then shalt thou call, and the LORD *shall answer; thou shalt cry, and he shall say, Here I am. If thou take away from the midst of thee the yoke, the putting forth of the finger, and speaking vanity;*

10 And if thou draw out thy soul to the hungry, and satisfy the afflicted soul; then shall thy light rise in obscurity, and thy darkness be as the noonday:

11 And the LORD *shall guide thee continually, and satisfy thy soul in drought, and make fat thy bones: and thou shalt be like a watered garden, and like a spring of water, whose waters fail not."*

Law of the fast: Fasting helps us come closer to God and help fight off evil. It requires sacrifice and consecration. The Savior teaches that to build Zion we must eliminate individual tendencies to selfishness. We must cooperate completely and work in harmony with one another. There must be oneness in decision-making and activities. We must unite in prayer with all the energy of our hearts.

Fasting two meals: My mother taught me to fast for twenty-four hours. However, she is now 94 years old and it is difficult for her to fast that long. Too often, the fast begins after a late Saturday night party or on Sunday morning when we are reminded that it is Fast Sunday. The Spirit of fasting helps us control our appetites and refrain from self-gratification.

Fasting with a purpose, prayer, and commitment: We fast to:

1. Gain inner strength, power and wisdom
2. Pray with a purpose
3. To overcome temptation
4. To achieve success
5. To humble and prepare ourselves
6. To develop commitment to act

Brothers and sisters, you have heard the mind and will of the Lord regarding fasting, fast offerings and the spirit of the fast. This past week, my wife chose to call it the Eternal Revenue Service. In fact, that is just what it is.

11.

GRADUATION OR CELEBRATION?

Learning Never Ends

Upon graduation from a university, real-life learning just begins. Your diploma is your ticket to travel the world of reality. It is your tuition for the first semesters of gaining real-world experience. Today, this phase of your formal education is over, but your real learning will now begin.

You all have dreams to follow and goals to achieve. You have good intentions and care about doing great things and making a difference in the world. Perhaps you feel that you have everything all figured out, but I hope to give you some important ideas to think about.

You are responsible. You're young and have vigor and something to prove. You thrive on self-empowerment and want to make a difference in the world.

Achieve Your Destiny

Don't get discouraged when you come face to face with reality. As you feel the cold winds blowing in your face and down your back, button up and keep going. You will occasionally slip or stumble because of inexperience. You will get knocked down a few times by rejection. It happens to everyone, and it will happen to you. Don't be afraid. Be determined and be strong.

Failures stay down. Great people get up and keep going. So get up and dust yourself off. Remember that the world needs you and is depending on you to be successful and achieve your greatness. There are problems to be solved and discoveries to be made. There is truth and justice to be defended. There is service to be rendered and sacrifices to be made. There are a lot of beginners, but the world needs you to be finishers.

There are times of discouragement for everyone. In those moments we may feel forgotten or even forsaken. We must be patient and know that things will work out in the end. God will not abandon us nor forsake us. He may be testing us or giving us an opportunity to grow and become strong. We need to have faith and be patient to see the impossible become reality.

Do not quit! Do not accept defeat! Failure is not an option!

Choose to Be Great

Perhaps you did not want to have some of the bad things happen in your life, but you can choose how to respond to these bad things. Your choice will make the difference of whether you are a champion or a failure. No matter what your situation or stature, you can choose to be "who" and "what" you want to be. You can be great if you choose to be and if you are willing to pay the price of greatness. If you want to be great, you must think like a great person thinks. You must speak and act like a great person. You must be a great person.

Think Great

Do not entertain negative thoughts. Do not allow evil thoughts or images to enter your mind or heart. Think the best of yourself and the best of others. We all make mistakes, but we all have Divine potential. All of your instincts, desires, appetites and passions can be developed into great and noble qualities of character and happiness. They all can also be perverted and decay into ugly, base and evil qualities that will destroy and cause sadness and misery. It is your choice, and your choice alone that decides on what you will do with your challenges and opportunities.

Speak Great

Choose your words carefully. Craft your thoughts in sentences that are descriptive. They don't have to be eloquent to be meaningful and powerful. Use great language to persuade and influence. Use vocabulary that is enlightening and empowering. Use your speech to lift and inspire.

At times, when you speak the truth with nobility and clarity, you might be derided and belittled. You might be accused of hatred, bigotry and racism. Your sanity and patriotism will be questioned, and everything you hold dear may be insulted and attacked. Nevertheless, if you are to be great, speak with the heart of a teacher to persuade others to consider the principles and ideas you share.

Act Great

Respect everyone, especially your parents and family. Be courteous at all times. Be protective of individuals and their personal rights. Don't get caught up in the trap of group thinking or peer pressure. To be great, you must choose to stand in the right place, and then stand firm. Compromise is for the marketplace of things. There can be no compromise in the marketplace of truth and ideals.

Individuals or Groups

Don't let society convince you that their groups need your attention and resources. Choose your own special group, or groups, and use your energy and ability to act to protect individuals and individual rights. Keep your identity and focus on individuals, and not on group dynamics. This will make all the difference in your ability to succeed. Groups often get the idea that they have rights because of popularity or need. They sometimes come to believe that individuals should sacrifice for the cause of the group and do what they can to impose their thinking to get their own way. Individuals have the right to protect their lives and their property from the plunder of the masses.

Group Mentality

Your past formal educational environment focused a lot on developing a group mentality. You classes, clubs, or teams all helped mold you into a group. Be careful not to be caught up in the wrong kind of groups. Don't look to someone else to provide for you and give you security. Be self-reliant. Look to provide for yourself. You can and must develop your own individual identity. In summary, be the master of your fate and the captain of your soul.

Be Loyal

There are some groups that you should always stay loyal to, including your family, church, community and nation. However, you will notice that your diploma has only your name on it. Once you find yourself and discover your own greatness, it is very difficult to back to a group mentality. You may have to in order to pay the bills and feed your family, but sooner or later, you will have to be your own boss and make things happen. Ultimately, we are responsible for ourselves.

Different Kinds of People

It's been said that there are three kinds of people;

1. A few who make things happen;
2. Spectators who watch things happen; and
3. A whole lot of people who just wonder what happened!

Benjamin Franklin said, "All mankind is divided into three classes: those that are movable, those that are immovable, and those that move."

Then there is a group who would like to silence everybody and have everyone go along to get along. Someone has to be willing to stand up to such bullies.

Be careful and choose your friends carefully. The people you associate with will affect your thinking, speaking and behavior. You will probably marry one of them. You might start a business or go to work for some of them. These people will help and guide you along the way to greatness, or they will slow you down, detour, or stop you. Choose carefully!

A Sure Partner

The old saying goes, "Two things are for sure – death and taxes." If you live a good life, you won't ever have to worry about dying. But, as soon as you begin earning money, your "sure lifetime partner" will want his share. If it hasn't already happened, your eyes will be opened, and you will become intimately acquainted with "Uncle Sam." He won't help you be successful. He will not share in your efforts. He will just sit back and wait for his share of your earnings.

This partner will be the federal government. It claims to be your agent, but in reality it is the agent for the recipients for every government program that has been created. Uncle Sam will take your money so he can give it to teenage mothers bearing children out of wedlock. He will give your money to struggling artists and scientists who want to research novel ideas. He will give your money to people who would rather have you pay their bills. The government, however, has no constitutional authority to do any of this.

Some of your money will go to foreign government officials in the form of foreign aid. Little of this money reaches the people in need. He will give it to multinational corporations so their officers can have big bonuses. Some of it will go to elected officials working as your public servants. These officials have voted themselves pay raises and benefits that they cannot find anywhere else in the world. Your government will be a partner who tells you what you can and cannot do.

Gifts of Burden

Believe it or not, this powerful and oppressive government group has become a legal agent with legal power to use force, including deadly force, to accomplish its goals. It has many goals, one of which is for you to pay your fair share of a growing national debt that it created while you were still in diapers. The debt grew to unimaginable size while you were studying so you could go out and start your own company or get a good job and buy the "stuff" you wanted to have.

Whether you like it or not, you are bound with the chains of this debt. You are bound with the chains of responsibility to provide for all the needy and less fortunate and clean up after others and restore every disaster in America and around the world. This is not voluntarily giving charity. This is what someone else sees as goodwill imposed on you.

Agent of Plunder

Your partner is an agent of plunder. The more you succeed, the more he takes. You can still be great and do noble things, but your new learning environment will be very different from your old classrooms. You can choose to like being plundered, but I believe the federal government has stepped way out of bounds of its constitutional limits.

My grandparent's generation gave my parents a nation of freedom and opportunity.

My parents' generation gave us:

1. The 16th and 17th Amendments to the constitution (income tax & less state representation);
2. Social Security; and 3) Medicare.

Our generation has forgotten God and is giving you immorality, a bloated national debt, and a bloated federal government.

If I were an advocate of these things, I would just put in my order for three square meals a day, my own TV with unlimited channels, and enough money to spend the winters in Arizona or Florida and my summers in Maine, Minnesota, or Montana. I want lots of fresh vegetables and fresh seafood, and please get my mail to me before 10:00 a.m. Well, I'm not an advocate of these government social programs, so I've planned and worked hard to take care of myself. I'm in the same boat you are, and I have to help solve all these problems so we don't end up with some other country owning or controlling us.

Fear and Control Government

It is my goal to inspire you to fear government and to vigilantly control it, as designed by our U.S. Constitution. You should fear it and learn to control it or it will control you. Government is necessary and good if feared and controlled by the people. If it is not feared and controlled, it will grow to proportions that are almost uncontrollable. Wrestling back the control could cost many lives and huge resources.

Fabricated Rights

There has been an obscene explosion of so-called "rights." Someone has fabricated the right to have a job; the right to a place to live; the right to a certain wage; the right to health care; and the right to education. Gradually, pets are having more rights than people.

These are not rights; these are wants or wishes. People may think they have these rights, but they don't. We only have a right to live free. We have no right to any portion of the life or liberty of another person. You have no right to the time, life or experience of a doctor unless you pay him and he agrees to the deal. You have no right to demand someone give you a job or compensate you unless they want to.

You do have a right to be homeless, unemployed, dirty, drunk or overdosed on drugs. You may be poor, ill or unfortunate due to a disaster. But, you have no right to demand others to accommodate you or solve your problems. That is your choice and responsibility. It is their choice to be compassionate and to help and serve, but it is not constitutional for the government to force anyone to be compassionate, to help, or to serve.

Choice and Responsibility

Success and failure are not a matter of good fortune or bad luck. If success equals luck, then why try. If failure means bad fortune, then it's fate, and there is nothing we can do about it.

Do not believe this type of thinking. Do not gamble with your life. Your future depends on the choices you make and the responsibilities you accept and keep. My father always warned me to, "Be careful with what you want because you are likely to get it." You must use your power to choose wisely—very wisely.

Each of us is where we are because of the choices we have made. There are also outside factors which can have a strong influence on our choices, but we choose how we react to these factors and influences. When disease, disaster or deprivation causes some to fall or fail, it is our choice to stand by and watch or reach out and help. That is our individual right to choose, not the government's right to force us to do what they think is best. Individuals have this right, but the government has assumed this right. It is now for you to make your choice for today and for the future.

If others insist that something be done, encourage and support them in their efforts. Applaud them for their donation of time, money and work, and give your time, money and work alongside them. But do not let them use government power to force you to do something that they should do themselves. Let them know that you recognize and will respond to the problem. Let them know that you are donating and working in your own way as they are in theirs.

Personal Responsibility

Personal choices lead to success or failure. If we accept responsibility for our choices, we have a much better chance of succeeding than if we try to hold others responsible.

You choose what you think and say. You choose your friends and how you act. You choose the movies you see and what you watch on TV or on the Internet. You choose what you read. You choose to have sex outside of marriage or remain chaste until and during marriage. You choose to speed or obey the law. You choose to consume alcohol or use drugs. You choose to save your money or to burden yourself with debt. These choices determine who you are and where you will be in the future.

Bad things will happen to you. This is part of life. Expect it, and make the most out of it. You *can* succeed and be happy.

Do Not Covet

Be thankful for what you have. Be happy for what others have. Don't fret over what you don't have. If something is missing, set goals and go for it. Develop an abundance mentality and help others progress on their path to success. The more people you help, the happier you will be.

Avoid envy, because it will only cause you to feel inadequate and unhappy. It doesn't matter what others have or how popular they are. It doesn't matter what others think or do to make themselves feel good. What matters is that you know who you are and that you have great worth. What matters is that you are spiritually and emotionally healthy.

When envy moves from the individual to the community or nation, people become polarized and begin to accuse one another and blame one another for everything that is wrong with the world. Anyone who envies loses. Poor people and their sponsors are bound in poverty. They rob themselves of opportunities to serve and help others. They fall deeper into self-pity and blame. Everyday people make choices that pull their families apart and create barriers for happiness. Rich and famous people do foolish things and lose their integrity and fortunes.

You Can Succeed and Be Great!

Do the things that successful people do. Think and speak the things that great people think and say. Do the things that great people do. Be great like other great people. Keep it up, and don't let up, because if you do the things failures do, you, too, will fail. If you think and say what failures think and say, you will begin to believe the lies they have bought into, and you will fall. Don't be a failure. Be a winner!

The Poverty Scam and Insensitivity

Poverty has very little to do with the amount of income you have, but it has a lot to do with what you do with what you have. Poverty is a government definition that creates a class of people. There are actually wealthy people who fall into class by definition. They participate in this scam of poverty and receive government support.

The government is creating "poverty prisons" for many who do not want to be there. No matter who you are, if you accept this definition, you are allowing the government or others to try and convict you without due process. You are admitting to crimes you didn't commit. You are admitting to being what they say you are. If you do this, you are checking yourself into the "poverty prison" and will remain in your cell until you decide to escape.

One of the reasons politicians and government bureaucrats promote a war on poverty is so they can appeal to the sympathy and compassion of good people who want to help. Soon, these good people begin to think that government, instead of individuals, should solve the problem. Social welfare programs expand government power, influence, and justification for their existence.

There would be more charitable service and more personal growth and social strength without a big government telling everyone what to do and how to do it. Without government meddling, people learn to get along better, solve problems faster, and do great things.

Challenge

I challenge you to consider these ideas and put them to the test. We've tried the social engineering and welfare programs for over fifty years, and we are now producing more government dependence and putting more people into poverty prisons than ever before in the history of our nation.

I also challenge you to get involved in the political process. I challenge you to run for office or be involved in every election. Don't be a spectator. Be willing to get into the arena and participate. There are many ways to serve and support, but someone also needs to be willing to serve others as their representative and public servant. Ask God for help. God will guide you to know if it is for you to lead or support other good people in leading.

I challenge you to vote. You must register to vote, so get registered. Before you vote, do your homework. Compare the candidate's life and message against the Constitution. Ask God for guidance. He will help guide you to know who is speaking the truth and who to vote for.

I challenge you to not look to other's money to solve problems or to allow the government to be used as an instrument of plunder. If it is wrong for you to take by force from someone else who earned it, it is wrong for the government to do so. What you earn is yours, and what others earn is theirs. Nobody owes you anything except respect, privacy and your rights afforded by the Constitution of the United States.

I challenge you to think wisely and make good decisions. I challenge you to speak wisely. I challenge you to act wisely. I challenge you to be wise, and to be great!

12.

GRANDFATHER THORNTON ON MISSIONS

In 1902, my Grandfather, William Thornton, went with a friend to hear the Mormon missionaries preach on a street corner in a small coal mining town in Leeds, England. He had gone there to heckle the "Brighamites." Instead, he felt the spirit of the missionaries' testimonies and message. His friend, however, had a contentious spirit, so when my grandfather confronted him, the friend got upset and left. Grandfather chose to stay and listen to the elders. He was soon baptized and was promptly thrown out of his house and told never to return. He was nineteen years old. He married and brought his wife, also a convert, to gather with the Saints in Utah.

During the course of his life, Grandfather Thornton served five full-time missions and almost as many stake missions. Almost always he had to leave his wife and family of what was eventually seven small children to fend for themselves. But, he responded to the call of the prophet and enthusiastically shared the Gospel with everyone. Through his efforts and example, thousands have been converted.

In her eighties, my Aunt Elsie said how badly she felt about never having a father at home. She once chastised the Apostle Joseph Fielding Smith for this. He said, "Some were intended to be great fathers and others great missionaries. The Lord needed your father." After this response, Brother Smith invited her to use his office as long as she needed to, to ask the Lord for forgiveness for her feelings. In those days many members were on a very personal basis with the brethren.

Whatever his shortfall as a father, the family has kept the faith. Through my mother, just one of his children, there have been born under the covenant five of his grandchildren and over twenty great-grandchildren. All have married in the temple, and most have served missions. They are continuing to follow his example.

On one occasion during his last foreign mission, just after World War II, Grandfather was told in a letter by his Mission President, Hugh B. Brown, that Grandfather was being sent on another mission. President Brown wrote, "I am sending you on a mission to Hell, I mean Hull." For those who don't know, Hull, England, was severely bombed during the war. My grandparents, in their later years, were the first missionary couple to go into Hull after the end of World War II.

Another day, while my Grandmother was in their missionary apartment fixing something to eat, Grandfather approached a priest on the sidewalk. He cleverly dropped his copy of the Book of Mormon on the ground. The priest hurried over to help this little, old, white-haired man. Making sure the priest had noticed the title of the book, Grandpa turned around and walked with him. In fifteen minutes, when they arrived at the church where the priest served as the director of genealogical records, he had a testimony. Believing the words of Elder Thornton, he turned in his ministerial cloak and collar and left to be baptized. To my knowledge, his brother still lives with his wife and family in Alberta, Canada, and serves as the director of genealogical research for the LDS church there. I summary, Grandfather was always helping and giving, sharing his testimony or a copy of the Book of Mormon, or encouraging a discouraged missionary or convert. His legacy lives on.

13.

HARD HEARTS

The Bible Is the Word of God

I testify that the Bible is the word of God. It consists of the teachings of ancient prophets who were called of God to lead his people. They spoke and wrote as they were inspired by the Holy Ghost. The Old Testament prophets testified of the Messiah who would come to redeem his people. They foretold that he would be born of a virgin and that he would be crucified and resurrected. They obeyed God and sacrificed burnt offerings in similitude of the great sacrifice of the only begotten of the Father. The New Testament prophets and apostles testified of his birth, life and ministry. They testified that he lives, and that it was by the Holy Spirit that believers could come to know that he lives and that his Gospel is true.

Wicked Men Rejected Christ

Many Jews were hard hearted and despised Christ's words of plainness. They crucified the Son of God, killed the prophets and apostles, and persecuted the true believers. They were blind and deaf to the truth. They rejected Jesus Christ and revelation through the Holy Spirit because they were unwilling to give up the "law" as written in the Old Testament. They were a wicked people who used the law to justify the way they wanted to live. Christ loved them, taught them the truth, and invited them to follow him. They rejected the living Christ before and after he was resurrected, and they rejected the only way they could know him and his doctrine, which was revelation by the Holy Spirit (see Matthew 16:16-17 and James 1:5).

Need for Humility

Unless we humble ourselves and become as little children, we cannot enter into the Kingdom of Heaven (see Matthew 18:1-4). It is when we cultivate Christ-like attributes that we can understand and be like him. If we choose to hold fast to "the law" and harden our hearts and cover our sins we cannot progress. If we do this, we will not be open to the Spirit, to God's earthly messengers, to Divine messengers and angels, or even to the resurrected Christ himself. Even some of his chosen apostles could not believe until they touched the wounds in his hands and side.

Invitation

I invite you to open your mind, soften your heart, and hear the words of the living Christ. I invite you to repent of your sins, stop justifying sinning, and come unto him. Walk in his path and seek not to council the Lord in what he can or cannot do. I testify that he lives. He knows and loves you personally. He desires for you to "seek, ask, and knock" and "find, receive, and enter" to enjoy the fullness of his Gospel. I also testify that there is false doctrine being taught by false prophets, and evil spirits who can appear as angels of light (see Matthew 24:23-24). I also testify that there are true prophets and divine messengers from God declaring his word today as in ancient times.

Christ promises, protects, and respects your agency to choose between good and evil. Lucifer/Satan wants to take way your agency and will do anything to deceive you, including the lie that God does not speak to man through prophets or the Holy Spirit anymore. Satan teaches that the gifts of the Spirit were only at the time of Pentecost. He teaches that miracles have ceased, and no one can add to or subtract from Bible. If that were so, then everything after Deuteronomy would have to be rejected (Deuteronomy 4:2). This applies to all scripture forbidding us to not change the revelations of God. This does not prohibit God from speaking to prophets or revealing his word through the Holy Spirit (see Revelations 22:18-19).

Baptism for the Dead

Baptism for the dead was taught as part of the Savior's Gospel and it was being practiced in New Testament times. When Paul was speaking to the Corinthians, some were struggling with the concept of resurrection (see I Cor. 15:12). Paul testified to them of the risen Christ, and explained that every person would be resurrected (see I Cor. 15:20-22). He then asked them why they baptized for the dead, if the dead were not resurrected.

Jesus Christ and his apostles also taught that, at the time of death, the spirits of all people go to a place to await the resurrection. On the cross, Christ told one of the thieves next to him, "Today shalt thou be with me in Paradise," which is a place for the righteous to dwell until the resurrection (Luke 23:43). Christ did go there and organize his work to take his Gospel to everyone who has ever lived on the earth. He also went to a place where the disobedient dwell called the "spirit prison." With his valiant and authorized representatives, he taught them his Gospel as described in I Peter 3:18-20.

Teaching Continues in the Next Life

When we die, we will also have the opportunity to teach about Jesus Christ and his Gospel to those who have not had the opportunity in this life. Because baptism is essential for them to enter the Kingdom of God (John 3:5), baptisms are now, and will be, performed for every person who has ever lived on the earth. This is done vicariously (for and in behalf of) for each person. Each person will have the opportunity to accept or reject this ordinance. No one will be forced to accept it, but the saving ordinance of baptism will be done for everyone.

Caution

God loves all of his children. Be careful not to be like the wicked of old and reject the living Christ and the fullness of his Gospel. I hope you won't spend your life trying to correct those "poor mislead Mormons" by politely listening so you can then say, "I've listened, and now it's my turn to speak."

I testify that the Spirit of the Holy Ghost will come upon you, and you will know more strongly than if you physically touched Christ's hands or heard his voice. His Gospel has been restored in these last days through living prophets. There are living on the earth today twelve apostles who know the resurrected Jesus, as did his original twelve. Their purpose is to testify that he lives, and that they lead his church to prepare the world for his second coming.

14.

HOLY SPIRIT

The Church of Jesus Christ of Latter-day Saints is led by Jesus Christ himself. He directs it through a living prophet and twelve apostles. You may have heard of us referred to as "Mormons," "LDS," or "Latter-day Saints." We also refer to ourselves by these names, but there is no "Mormon" church. It is The Church of Jesus Christ of Latter-day Saints. A saint is a member of the church, or a disciple of Christ. When a person is baptized and confirmed a member of the church, he or she receives the Gift of the Holy Ghost.

The Thirteenth Article of Faith says, "We believe in God the Eternal Father, in his son Jesus Christ, and in the Holy Ghost." The other names that sometimes refer to the Holy Ghost are Holy Spirit, Spirit of God, Spirit of the Lord, Comforter, Spirit of Truth, and Spirit. The Holy Ghost is the third member of the Godhead and is a personage of spirit, not possessing a body of flesh and bones. The Holy Ghost has been manifested to all mankind since Adam both as a POWER and as a GIFT.

All Have Felt His Influence

Everyone born on the earth has a conscience and instinctively senses the difference between good and evil. This is called the Light of Christ. However the Holy Ghost goes beyond this sense. This power can come before baptism, and is a convincing witness of truth. By the power of the Holy Ghost, a person receives a testimony of Jesus Christ and his work and the work of his servants on the earth. People from all over the earth, of every age, race and religion feel the power of the Holy Ghost at some time or other in their lives. I'm sure that each of you have had such an experience at some time in your life.

However, the Gift of the Holy Ghost comes only after faith, repentance and a properly authorized baptism. It comes after a person has searched and worked to draw closer to God. Jesus said, "Ask and ye shall receive. Seek and ye shall find. Knock and it shall be opened unto you." The Lord's invitation is to hear his message and find out if it is true.

When a person speaks by the power of the Holy Ghost, that same power carries a conviction of the truth to the heart of the hearer. The Holy Ghost knows all things and can help us to know all things. For the rest of your life, you can call upon the Holy Ghost to guide you, give you comfort and to help you understand many treasures of knowledge. He will guide you to the Savior and give you a sure knowledge that He is your Savior and the Redeemer of the World. You can enjoy this great blessing because of the restoration of the Gospel.

Laying on of Hands

This gift is conferred upon a person by the laying on of hands, as it was in Biblical times. After the baptism, the person who was just baptized sits in a chair, surrounded by men—often a father, uncles, and friends—who hold the Priesthood of God. They place their hands on the person's head while one man gives an official prayer, followed by a blessing.

Joseph Smith

It all began in New York, 1820, when Joseph Smith wanted to know what church he should join. He read in James 1:5-6: "If any of you lack wisdom, let him ask of God, that giveth to all men liberally, and upbraideth not; and it shall be given him."

Joseph said, "Never did any passage of scripture come with more power to the heart of man than this did at this time to mine."

Joseph later went to a grove of trees near his home and knelt in prayer. He said, "I saw a pillar of light exactly over my head, above the brightness of the sun at noon day, which descended gradually until it fell upon me . . . . When the light rested upon me I saw two personages, whose brightness and glory defy all description, standing above me in the air. One of them spake unto me, calling me by name, and said, pointing to the other, 'This is My Beloved Son, hear him!'" I testify that Joseph Smith saw Heavenly Father and Jesus Christ.

Restoration of Priesthood Power

In answer to his question about which church to join, Joseph was told to join none of them. Christ told him that He would restore his church on the earth. Seven years later, on May 15, 1827, John the Baptist came as a heavenly messenger and gave Joseph the authority to baptize. This was the same John the Baptist who had baptized Jesus Christ in the Jordan River. A short time later, Peter, James, and John (Christ's three chief apostles) gave Joseph the authority to give the Gift of the Holy Ghost and to organize the church.

If you choose to accept the Gospel, and be baptized and confirmed, the Holy Ghost will guide you and help you to make good decisions.

There are many ways that you can discern the influence of the Holy Spirit.

When You Have the Spirit

- You feel happy and calm.
- You feel full of light.

- Your mind is clear.
- Your heart burns with love for the Lord.
- You gladly and willingly perform church work.
- You feel like praying and reading the scriptures.
- You wish you could keep all the Lord's commandments all the time.
- Nobody can offend you.
- You feel confident in what you do.
- You feel generous.
- You are very forgiving and kind.
- You are glad when others succeed.
- You want to help others toward heaven.
- You say only the best about others.
- You feel a deep desire to help others—often in a way no one else will know about.
- You feel sorry when others have problems, and you sincerely desire to help them.
- You don't mind anyone seeing what you are doing.
- You feel you have control of your appetites and emotions.
- You realize that your thoughts and your actions are open to God.

I testify that this is true. This is God's work and his glory.

15.

HUAYCO EN HUANUCO: A MISSIONARY LESSON

Description of Peru

Peru is a beautiful country with a variety of people, cultures and climates. There are the very rich and the very poor. Lima is a large metropolitan city with over 7 million inhabitants, but most of Peru's population lives in smaller cities and villages, where many families still live in adobe houses and farm by hand or with oxen, just as their ancestors have done for centuries.

The west coast of Peru is a desert about 20 miles wide and stretches south from Ecuador to the border of Chile. The western slopes of the Andes Mountains are dry and rugged. They rise from sea level to over 16, 000 feet over the Ticlio Pass, the highest railroad pass in the world. The Andes Mountains get their name from the *andeas,* or terraces, built by the ancient Incas for agricultural purposes.

The high mountain plains are called the *Alti-plano* and look as if the whole area had been lifted up. The eastern slopes of the Andes are covered with vegetation and waterfalls cascading off the tops of high mountains. The best way to describe this beautiful land is to say that it looks very much like Arnold Freiburg's painting of Alma baptizing in the Waters of Mormon.

The eastern portion of Peru, which borders Brazil, is in the flat rainforest jungle where the headwaters of the Amazon River originate. As of 2014, there are 12 missions in Peru, with

776 congregations and one temple in operation and one under construction.

Doctrine and Covenants 49:24 predicts that "the Lamanites will blossom as a rose." This prophecy is literally being fulfilled, and I am so grateful to have been a part of seeing it come to pass. Church President Spencer W. Kimball told us that we must harvest while the "tide is in" and while the spirit is moving over this people. The same kind of thing that happened in England and Scandinavia during the early days of the church is now happening in Peru and throughout Central and South America. This is their day!

A Missionary Discussion

Crossing the (*Huayco en Huánuco*) or Avalanche in Huánuco

Probably one of the best missionary discussions I ever saw in Peru was taught one Sunday on our way home from a conference in Huánuco. I call it, "*Sacando su burro del barro en el día de reposo.*" In English that means, "Pulling your donkey out of the mire on the Sabbath."

Soon after leaving the city, we came upon a long line of traffic backed up from the night before because an *huayco,* or avalanche, had covered the road. There was a mudslide about two feet deep, and a line of over fifty buses full of people on both sides that had been waiting for many hours. It was Sunday, and there were no bulldozers to help. A large bus and a small Toyota pickup had both tried to cross, and both were stuck in the middle of the mud. The bus finally got out, but the pickup couldn't move. It had been there for hours.

There were more than 300 people on both sides of the road watching the driver try to dig the boulders out from in front of the wheels, but no one was helping him. Immediately, two LDS missionaries decided to go help this man and get things moving. They rolled up their shirtsleeves and waded into the knee-deep mud. Almost in chorus the spectators began to chide them and jeer at these two tall blond gringos in white shirts and ties. They hissed and booed and told the Mormons to "go home." They even threw rocks at them.

The elders just smiled and went to work. A silent hush came over the crowd as the elders dug out one boulder after another. With one great heave, they almost freed the vehicle. By this time the crowd began to believe that maybe the young men could get the job done. The whole feeling of the group changed from criticism to encouraging comments and compliments. Just then a drunken heckler stepped forward and threw a large boulder about the size of a grapefruit, which landed just a foot from the missionaries and splashed mud all over them. As he shouted some profanities, four or five men almost beat up the offender for having disrupted things. It was almost comical.

Then, with a final show of strength, the two elders literally lifted the back of the pickup out of the mud and over the last few boulders. As they pushed, the back wheels were spinning and throwing mud all over them. As they truck fish-tailed out, they jumped aboard and rode out of there like champions, with cheers and shouts from everyone. The crowd then ran back to their buses and cars to continue their journey.

We passed many of the buses as we traveled, and stopped to wash the mud out of our clothes in the river by the highway. As each bus passed by, they waved and cheered and thanked us. I am certain they will be more receptive when the missionaries knock on their doors in the future.

Kid in a Candy Store

When we arrived in Peru I felt like a kid in a candy store. It seemed like almost everyone was willing to listen to our message. It was nothing like New England, where I had served my first mission. For example, on one of our first trips to Tarma, high in the Andes Mountains, I met a young man as I was walking out of the hotel on my way to attend our evening leadership meetings. We visited for a few moments, and I gave him my card and a personal invitation to visit our new chapel and attend services. He knew nothing of the church, but he knew where the chapel was in the middle of town.

A month later, we returned to Tarma and were met at the chapel by the zone leaders, who immediately introduced us to one of their new contacts. Elder King told me I had invited him to come to church a month earlier. I then remembered the encounter, but did not recognize him as it had been dark the night we spoke in front of the hotel.

I asked him if the missionaries had taught him. He said, "Yes." I then asked him what he thought of their message. He responded, "I have gained a testimony, and I was baptized last night." I was thrilled.

Called to Serve

We are all called to serve. We are all missionaries, and we all have investigators to teach. Our wives and husbands and children are our most important investigators. We need to teach the Gospel to them in our homes, and we need to teach it by the spirit and power of the Holy Ghost.

We are all preparing to serve missions in the future. Some of us are preparing for our first mission at eighteen years of age for boys or nineteen years of age for girls. Others are preparing for missions later in life, with their husband or wife. We all can move the work forward now by preparing ourselves and our children. We can also contribute our financial resources as we have been invited and commanded to do.

Even little children can be missionaries. They are such great missionaries to us and to others and can pierce the hearts of many with their simple faith and pure testimonies.

When I served as mission president in Peru, my children were always eager to share a pamphlet with a stranger and tell someone about the church. They became quite involved and caught up in the mission and in living in Peru. They wanted to visit all the sights and ancient ruins. They became quite the archeologists. Once, while hosting a new mission president and his family, we visited the ancient ruins of Pachacamac just twenty minutes south of Lima. Of course, we were talking about the Book of Mormon and the Nephites and Lamanites as we pulled over to park and begin our walk. Immediately, the door to the van came open and the children jumped out and began to dig in the sand. As I walked around the front of the van, Jonathan stood up, holding up his first find. With excitement, he held up an old, broken and warped 45 rpm record and said, "Look what I found Dad!" Teresa Joy then shouted, "Look Dad, Jonathan found an ancient record!"

Just then Samuel came running over holding an old piece of broken bathroom tile and said, "Yah, but I found one of the glass plates!" Isn't it wonderful that we always find just what we are looking for?

16.

I-BEAM STORY

In the July 2009 *Ensign*, President Thomas S. Monson taught us about the worth of a soul. Using the analogy of the sugar beets that have fallen off the wagon, we learn that they have just as much sugar in them as those on the wagon. He said, "The sugar beets represent the members of this church . . . and those who have fallen out of the truck represent men and women, youth and children who, for whatever reason, have fallen from the path of activity . . . I say of these souls, precious to our Father and our Master: 'There's just as much value in those who have slipped off. Let's go back and get them . . . our mission is more than meetings. Our service is to save souls.'"

While working for the company Franklin Quest, I related the I-beam story many times to help people identify their governing values. We would ask if anyone had a child under the age of two to help us visualize and vicariously participate in the process of identifying and prioritizing governing values. This is not easy, but a very valuable experience. Here is the story:

Outside, we have an I-beam, 121 feet long. An I-beam is a steel beam used in the construction of tall buildings and other structures. It has a cross section that makes it looks like the capital letter "I." Its unique shape gives strength and rigidity. The I-beam is lying on the ground and stands about three feet high off the ground. It is about 18 inches wide across the top and bottom. I put you at one end, and I am on the other end.

I reach into my wallet and I pull out a $100 bill. If you walk across the I-beam without stepping off either side within two minutes, I will give you the money. Will you try? There is no real risk or danger, and almost anyone can do it.

Then we would change the scenario and say we were taking the I-beam to New York City to some very tall skyscrapers. The buildings are 120 feet apart, and we would hoist the beam to the top with a large crane and bolt it to each tower, overlapping 6 inches on each building. It's perfectly safe and will not fall.

You are on one building and I am on the other. I raise my $100 bill and say if you come across without stepping off either side within 2 minutes, I will give you the money. Will you come?

Change the scenario a little bit more. Now I have $10,000. It is yours the moment you step on my side. Will you come? Now I have $50,000, tax free. Will you walk over? I have a million dollars. The wind has come up a little, and a bit of rain falls, and the I-beam is bowed. The two buildings are swaying in unison.

Change the scenario. There is a very bad person next to me, and he has your child by the arms as the child is hanging over the edge. He says, "If you don't get across the I-beam right now, I will drop your child." Would you come?

We have identified one of your governing values. It is, "I love my child." Money is important. Safety is important. But of greater value is the love for my child. That is what governing values are all about.

Some parents of teenagers will not come across. Once in a while they will say, "Drop him!"

What would you cross the I-beam for? What idea, principle, or person, has such great value to me that I would risk, maybe even dedicate my life for it? What we are talking about is coming to grips with what matters most.

Perhaps we can't actually walk the I-beam for anyone. However, each of us can follow the Savior by doing what he would have us do. Prioritize our values. Make sure our values are in keeping with the teachings of Christ.

WORTH OF A SOUL

How many men have walked a mile,
One hundred or a thousand if need be,
To find their fortune, their glory or pride;
To conquer the mountain or sea?

How many have given life or limb,
Or a better part of their soul,
For a diamond, a treasure or even a purse,
Or a trophy for winning a goal?

If so many have run this kind of race
And paid the prices required,
Why haven't more helped others in need,
Instead of quitting when tired.

The worth of a soul is greater than all
The riches we all can combine.
This is the measure our Savior taught
As he left the ninety and nine.

Moral Courage—The Story of Esther

Let us have the moral courage to make our actions consistent with our knowledge of right and wrong.

In 3 Nephi 3:7 it says: "I will go and do the things that the Lord hath commanded, for I know that the Lord giveth no commandments unto the children of men, save he shall prepare a way for them that they may accomplish the thing which he commandeth them."

I know that once the Lord gives us a commandment we have the choice to follow through or choose our own path. One of my favorite examples of someone who showed moral courage is Esther, the Queen of Persia, in the Old Testament. She was a woman of pure integrity and love for her Jewish people. She had the courage to stand for truth and righteousness, although it meant placing her life in grave danger as she literally offered it up to save her people from execution. Here is the story:

When the King of Persia chose to marry Esther, an orphan, things looked bright. But, the king's counselor in the royal court hated the Jews. Esther's cousin, Mordecai, warned Esther never to reveal that she is Jewish. One day, the councilor, Haman, ordered Mordecai to bow down before him. Mordecai refused, saying he will only worship God. In retribution, Haman convinced the king that all of the Jews in the kingdom should be slain. All the Jews mourn and fast, asking God to save them. Esther, knowing her husband, the king, could have her killed for daring to approach him without being invited, asks to talk to him. Instead of being angry, the king is delighted to see her. Eventually, the evil and devious plot to kill the Jews is revealed, and the councilor is hanged on his own gallows.

A great hymn that keeps me in line when I am facing a challenging moral decision is "Do What Is Right." The chorus goes:

"Do what is right; let the consequence follow.
Battle for freedom in spirit and might;

And with stout hearts look ye forth till tomorrow.
God will protect you; then do what is right."
("Do What Is Right", Hymns of the Church of Jesus-Christ of Latter-day Saints, 237)

I know that if we have the courage to follow our Father in Heaven, the consequences in our life will bring us joy and lead our life in the right direction.

17.

MARRIAGE—AFTER YOUR MISSION

To all of you young missionaries, some advice about looking for the right person to marry after you return home. During your mission, you have been faithful to the "mission rules" of not dating, dancing, listening to music, going to movies, or being alone with anyone of the opposite sex. Soon you will be released, and with this release will come other opportunities, such as marrying in one of God's sacred temples. Your "plan" to accomplish this "goal" will, and should, include dating, dancing, listening to good music, going to good movies, and developing wholesome relationships with members of the opposite sex in order to make your choice of an eternal companion. This will be the most important decision of your life.

You will be wise to follow the counsel of President Spencer W. Kimball, who said, "Never marry unless it is in the temple of God to a righteous individual who will be better than you are and will stimulate you to the highest things. Go all over this church if you need to, to find the one who is better than you . . . You are looking for the mother [or father] of your children, for a wife (or husband) for eternity."

Let me share the following inspirational poem, entitled "That Special One." I received it during the second year after I returned from my first mission. It let me know that my search was worthy of my best efforts:

That Special One

But, as I travel the world, it's you that I'll find,
Not tarnished by others and then left behind.
But, far from the path when my searching is done,
I will sit down beside you my dear special one;
And nurture the love that God meant to be,
For you see, special one, you're that special to me.

Don't rush out and marry the first person you date or the first who shows interest, but don't wait too long either. Marry the right person, at the right time and in the right place.

Remember that your affections should be saved for your spouse and your passionate expressions of affections are to be shared only after you are legally married. President Kimball has counseled, "A kiss is an evidence of affection. A kiss is an evidence of love, not an evidence of lust—but it can be! Don't ever let a kiss in your courtship spell lust. Necking and petting are lustful; they are not love. . . . Will you remember that? I don't mind your kissing each other after you have had several dates. But not the 'Hollywood Kiss', not the kiss of passion, but the kiss of affection, and there won't be any trouble. Now, remember these things."

God has commanded that men and women should leave their parents when they marry and establish their own home (see Genesis 2:18, 24). As husband and wife and in partnership with God, you will be privileged to invite special children into your home as you share your sacred expressions of affections.

Remember that communication, service, and sacrifice are the key ingredients to developing eternal bonds of love between husband and wife. Ever be true to one another in every way before your marriage and for the rest of eternity.

18.

MARRIAGE—HOW TO IMPROVE YOUR MARRIAGE

Focus on service, and treat each other with respect and dignity. Get out once in a while and have some fun. On a regular basis, take a marriage inventory including: spiritual, emotional, physical, financial and educational goals and concerns. Regularly read the church's guide, "The Family, A Proclamation to the World."

1. **Learn to be happy with what you have** because if you don't, you will never be happy.
2. **Express love and show affection.**
3. **Be courteous.**
4. **Be your best for your best**. Do more than what is expected.
5. **Take good care of yourself.** Practice good hygiene, eating habits, and exercise. "Paint your barns and polish your brass." President Kimball
6. **Have fun!**

If Ever Two Were One

If ever two were one,
Then surely we can be.
So sacred is our love
For all the world to see.

Remember us in friendship?
Our hearts were wide awake.

We'd gladly give or sacrifice
For one another's sake.

We found a special oneness
In the Gospel plan,
And realized the meaning
Of woman, and of man.

With the Holy Spirit binding
All our thoughts and deeds,
Inspiring us with wisdom
And aiding in our needs.

Such oneness is a virtue,
Of this I am so sure;
That our Heavenly Parents
Share a love so sweet and pure.

It's true that we are human
And need humility,
But if our souls are one,
Like them, we too, will be.

It seems so very often
That the veil seems to part,
And glimpses of eternity
Bring praises to my heart.

It causes little wonderment
When I hear your tender voice,
Through space and distance whispering,
"Commune and come rejoice."

Yes, in spirit we're communing
Through the whole entire day,

And in our dreams at nighttime
We laugh and joke and play.

We feel each other's feelings,
Tasting the bitter and the sweet.
We sense the other's nearness
And often times we meet.

Oh God, bless our growing oneness,
Like Thee we wish to be.
If ever two were one,
Then surely we will be.

Elder Boyd K. Packer said that we never need to speak the first harsh words. This inspired me to write the following poem.

First Harsh Words

"The first harsh words never need to be spoken,"
Was the counsel to bride and groom.

They are Satan's tools that hurt and divide,
And bring to all, sorrow and gloom.

So resolve this day to bridle your tongue,
And never drive loved ones apart.

Only speak softness in loving tones,
The feelings and thoughts of your heart.

As we strive to prepare for the Second Coming of the Lord Jesus Christ, let us strive to improve our marriages.

"When a man hath taken a new wife, he shall not go out to war, neither shall he be charged with any business: but he shall be free at home one year, and shall cheer up his wife which he hath taken." Deut. 24:5.

19.

MARRIAGE—
WEDDING CEREMONY, REMARKS, AND COUNSEL

We have gathered here together to celebrate one of the most beautiful moments in the lives of a man and woman. To the bride and groom, and to all those who are in this room, I stand as a witness before you to declare to one and all that marriage is ordained of God, our Eternal Father, for his sons and daughters here on earth. It has been so from the beginning. It is part of God's plan for all his children and for the two of you.

It has always been God's plan to create families through marriage. Before they were married, Adam and Eve lived in the Garden of Eden. They were like little children and were innocent, not knowing good from evil. They were given two commandments. The first, and most important, was to multiply and replenish the earth. The second, was not to partake of the fruit of the tree of knowledge of good and evil. Adam and Eve couldn't keep both commandments. They had to break one to keep the other. There is an eternal law that requires opposition in all things.

The first parents were given their agency to choose. However, being innocent, they couldn't keep the greater commandment to have children until they gained knowledge. In an effort to separate Adam and Eve and to destroy and frustrate God's plan, Satan tempted them to partake of the fruit and become as God, knowing good from evil. Adam refused, but Eve was deceived and partook of the fruit. When Adam discovered this, Eve explained that she would be cast out of the garden and he would remain alone forever.

At this point, Adam had to make a choice. He chose to break one of God's commandments and partake of the fruit in order to keep the greater commandment and remain with Eve, and to multiply and replenish the earth.

By partaking of the fruit, Adam knowingly committed the first sin, and as a result, he brought physical death into the world. God said to Adam and Eve:

Although this sin that Adam and Eve committed affected all of us, we rejoiced because it was the only way we could all progress according to God's plan. Each time we witness a wedding, we remember our first parents and what they did for all of us, and that marriage is ordained of God. In Mark 10:6-8, the Savior said, ". . . from the beginning of the creation, God made them male and female. For this cause shall a man leave his father and mother, and cleave to his wife; and they twain shall be one flesh: so then they are no more twain, but one flesh. What therefore God hath joined together, let not man put asunder."

The Apostle Paul taught, ". . . neither is the man without the woman, neither the woman without the man, in the Lord. For as the woman is of the man, even so is the man also by the woman; but all things are of God" (1 Corinthians 11:11-12).

There is a special thought which outlines my counsel about marriage:

- Coming together is the beginning.
- Staying together is progress.
- Working together is unity.
- Thinking together is success.

I challenge you to discover the formula of success for your marriage. You are unique, and your formula will be unique to you. However, there are some principles that apply to every marriage and will help your marriage to be successful. They include: SERVICE, SACRIFICE, COMMITMENT, HARD WORK, and PATIENCE.

If you SERVE one another at all times, including in sickness and old age, you will grow to truly love one another.

If you SACRIFICE, willingly, your own interests or priorities for the other, you will grow to love one another.

If you COMMIT yourself, your heart, mind, and effort, and never turn back, you will grow to love one another.

If you WORK HARD and have PATIENCE with yourself and with one another, even when you don't want to or when it is the hardest thing to do, you will grow to love one another.

This is counsel that the Apostle Paul gave to young couples: "Let the husband render unto the wife due benevolence, and likewise also the wife unto the husband" (Ephesians 5:20-25).

As husband and wife, we can support one another. We can teach and learn from one another. We can grow with one another, and we can protect one another during times of difficulty, physical danger, false accusations, and temptation. Our spouse can serve as a voice of warning to us.

Some guidelines that we can follow in our marriages are as follows:

- Couples should emphasize their roles as a team.
- Couples should establish and maintain a bond of love and respect for each other.
- Couples need to find ways to serve one another.

- Couples should avoid becoming preoccupied with negative thoughts and concentrate of the positive. If we have the spirit of contention we will not have the spirit of the Holy Ghost. When small irritations arise we need to develop the characteristics of the Savior.
- Couples should make sure that any necessary correction is constructive and done in the right spirit.
- Husbands and wives must communicate honestly and frequently with each other.
- Husbands and wives must be loyal to one another and never share personal things with friends or family members.
- Spouses should obey the standards of conduct and the rules of the church. This will help them overcome temptations and avoid compromising moral laws. These laws are based on divine inspiration. Many serious problems can occur by foolish or negligent violation of simple common sense.
- Husbands and wives should be sensitive to their spouse's needs and challenges, and should provide or seek help when needed.
- When you have challenges, and you will have challenges, for there must need be opposition in all things, remember that God has given you one another to help you succeed.

If you do these things, you will have true love, and you will find ways to pass the tests that you will face. You will find joy and happiness in living, and you will fulfill your true measure of creation on this earth.

20.

MINISTERING TO MINISTERS

What specific things can we do to help our non-LDS friends come to Christ? Perhaps introduce them to the missionaries or invite them to attend church? But, are our friends ready for this? Perhaps the first thing we can do is to encourage them to pray and read the scriptures. When they say, "I'm Catholic or I'm Baptist, etc.," maybe we can introduce them to their own minister and help them take smaller, but very important steps more willingly.

Many wonderful people in the world feel they have been called by God to minister to his children. Perhaps we can assist these pastors to help bring their flocks closer to Christ and ultimately to the fullness of the Gospel. By helping them serve their flocks, we will view them less as competitors and more as someone doing their best with the light and knowledge they have.

Pastor Frank

While living in Connecticut, I helped raise money to build a sanctuary for a non-denominational church operating the New Hope Christian Academy where our children attended school. Pastor Frank once asked if I would answer a few questions. He explained that he grew up believing Mormon's were a cult. He was curious about several of our doctrines. I answered his questions, then paused and shared a thought that came to my mind. I said, "Pastor Frank, there are so many misconceptions about who Mormons are and what we believe. But, I can promise you that if you really understood what Mormon's believed, you'd want to be one."

Pastor August

More recently, I had a wonderful experience hosting Pastor Rick August of the Greater Grace Apostolic Assembly church in Biloxi, Mississippi. Some years ago, he left the Air Force and formed his own church with his family and four other individuals. His congregation has grown to over 200 members. For the past five or six years, they have rented the old Biloxi LDS Ward meetinghouse, which they have cared for as their own. Last month, Pastor August came to Salt Lake City to pay the rent, discuss possibly purchasing the building, which was now for sale, and to learn more about the Mormons.

In the Joseph Smith Memorial Building Distribution Center, I presented him with a copy of *True to the Faith* and a copy of the Book of Mormon. I said that I hoped he would not be afraid to read it. He said he was not afraid. After briefly explaining the Book of Mormon, I picked up a copy of *Jesus the Christ* and explained that it had been written by a modern-day Apostle and was one of the most comprehensive books about the Savior. He seemed very eager to read it.

He picked out two editions of *The New Era* and told me he had used our young missionaries as examples for his youth for not smoking, drinking, using drugs, or fighting. He had instituted Family Home Evening, but didn't really know any details. I gave him a copy of the FHE resource manual and a food storage manual to use along with the Provident Living section of the church's website, LDS.org. My final gift was a movie on DVD about the miracles of Christ. I invited him to show it to his congregation and promised that they would love it.

Objectives – Goals – Results

The objective of talking to ministers of other religions is to prepare these spiritually-oriented people to reject misconceptions about the LDS beliefs and people. Give them doctrine and resources to help them in their ministries to bless the lives of their congregations.

The goal of this idea is to help ministers, parents and individuals of other churches with the resources that will ultimately bring them to the full knowledge of the truth and build their faith in Jesus Christ.

The results will be more understanding, friendship and goodwill. Bible bashing with ministers will disappear. Our missionaries and general membership will look at ministers of all faiths as golden contacts instead of adversaries. They will see other congregations as their flocks. The work will go forward much faster from the inside than from the outside. When missionaries do knock on the doors of their members, we will be helping to spiritually strengthen their congregations instead of stealing away their numbers. The idea is to serve these leaders and help them bring their flocks to the truth and into the Gospel.

The Hour Is Late

The struggle between good and evil is intensifying, and the polarization of people is accelerating at an ever-increasing pace. We know we live in the late hours of the last days in preparing for the Second Coming of Jesus Christ. We are doing so many wonderful things that we pray will be acceptable to the Lord, but all of us feel a constant urge to bring more individuals, families, and groups unto Christ. Programs, technology and resources of the church have been and are being refined. Individual members, wards and stakes are being strengthened.

The bar of worthiness is being raised for missionaries and members. Temples and meeting facilities are abundant, and we are enjoying an increase in respect and acknowledgement from the world.

In ancient times and during the early days of the Restoration, many ministers led their congregations to the truth. Today we enjoy increased respect from the world, but there is still so much we can do.

21.

MISSIONARY WORK: EVERYONE CAN DO IT

Helping Hands

In the last General Conference, President Dieter F. Uchtdorf told of a large statue of the Savior in Germany that was damaged by heavy bombing during World War II. The hands had been damaged beyond repair and could not be restored. So the people of the city added a sign on the base of the statue. The sign read, "You are my hands." President Uchtdorf pointed out that Jesus loved all people, ministered to them, and offered hope and salvation. This is what He would do today if He were here. President Uchtdorf said this is what we should also be doing. "As we emulate his perfect example, our hands can become his hands; our eyes, his eyes; our heart, his heart."

Teach Everyone

Referring to the scriptures, the Lord said in D&C 42:58, "And I give unto you a commandment that then ye shall teach them unto all men; for they shall be taught unto all nations, kindreds, tongues and people." We are to teach the masses in the world, and we are to teach each individual in the world.

Missionary Program

Brothers and Sisters, the full-time missionaries are here to help us fulfill our responsibilities. The Savior has taught the prophets, and the prophets have taught us that we as members are here to find and prepare people to hear the message of the restored Gospel. The missionaries are called to teach, to testify and to baptize those we find. We provide the referrals and we fellowship. We invite our friends to follow Christ. We are his hands, his eyes, and his heart. We are preparing for the Savior's Second Coming. Our efforts will determine what he finds when he comes.

Hugh Nibley

Recently, a book came out about Hugh Nibley's wartime experiences. As a young missionary in Germany just before World War II broke out, he went from house to house and store to store to warn the people that if they did not repent, they would be destroyed by fire from heaven. That was the message for them at that time. He found little interest and even stiff opposition to his message, but he was valiant in proclaiming that message. He later had to go back to Germany and fight in the war and see his own words fulfilled as the German people were destroyed by fire from bombs dropped from the skies.

Africa

There are many exciting missionary stories of how the church is growing in African countries. One account is about a South African church member who accompanied Elder Jeffrey Holland to Ethiopia. While talking to the missionaries in Ethiopia Elder Holland said, pointing to everyone in the group, "Like Paul, perhaps some of you may suffer and be thrown in prison for the Gospel's sake."

The next day while checking in at the airport, the South African brother was detained and thrown in jail for three and a half weeks. Later, this man reported that Elder Holland had been prophetic in his message. He also wanted to assure them that he had taught the Gospel every day while in prison. What an exciting missionary story he can tell his children and grandchildren.

The Vision

What if the Savior came here today and said, "Brothers and Sisters of the Trenton, Missouri, Branch, you are so very special. I know each of you individually and I love you personally. I have a work for you to do. Please share the Gospel with the people within the borders of the Trenton Branch. There are hundreds whom I have prepared, and there are thousands more for you to prepare to enter the waters of baptism. It is my desire and challenge for you to create the Trenton Missouri Stake."

Now some of you might doubt this and you may hear yourself saying, "Well, that won't happen for many years." If you think such thoughts, you can rest assured that they are not from the Lord. Do not let doubt stop you from acting for the Lord.

Airport Missionaries

I was going through the screening and check-in lines in the Salt Lake City Airport last Monday. There were quite a few missionaries ahead of me, and I was enjoying watching and listening to them. Some were going to various parts of the United States. Others were going to Hungary and Asia. Some of the missionaries seemed a little tired because it was early in the morning. Some looked timid, or maybe they were just missing the MTC or their family. One tall elder and his companion really had the missionary spirit. They were going to the Sacramento California Mission. They talked to everyone, and everyone knew who they were, where they were going, and what they were going to do when they got there. I could actually feel their enthusiasm and faith.

Guests at Marydale Inn

This past week, my wife Mary-Jo and I hosted several couples as guests at our Marydale Inn, the bed-and-breakfast we run. One was from the Community of Christ church, so the conversation allowed Mary-Jo to share a copy of the Book of Mormon. When I walked in, Mary-Jo was reading the 89th section of the D&C to our six guests. Wow, was I proud of her! She sent the guests on their way to Nauvoo. They had never heard of these things before and were not planning on a trip to Nauvoo, but they went to hear about the restored Gospel and the story of the pioneers. Who knows, some day people may be telling the story of "Grandma Jo, the Fighting Inn Keeper." If she wins, they hear the Gospel. If she loses, they get to stay the night for free!

What Holds Us Back?

What holds us back? With God, all things are possible. Without God, all things are just hard work! Why don't we do missionary work? Are we ashamed of the Gospel? Is it our pride? Is there some sin that needs to be taken care of? Is it because we do not have a testimony? Are we afraid?

We are all investigators on the road to exaltation. Some have not yet found the truth, others have had the discussions and been baptized. We are all trying to progress and endure to the end. A big part of our progress in learning to become like God depends on sharing what we have.

Lenny Ralphs, Dottie's husband, told me that, in some places, the Family Search assistants are having 4 times the success in live convert baptisms as the traditional proselyting missionaries are having. Get together with the Lord, find your way, and share the Gospel!

Invitation and Promise

Brothers and Sisters, missionary work is enjoyable, and you can do it. It's being yourself. It's being a Christian. It's helping someone with their genealogy. It's helping at the thrift store. It's helping them fix their car or serving them as a waitress or policeman. It's not just when you knock on doors, when you feed the missionaries, or stand on a box on a crowded street corner and call people to repentance. It's just everyday living.

I invite you to be anxiously engaged in missionary work as a part of your daily life. I plead with you to do specific things for the Lord. I share with you the Lord's command to stand as a witness in all times and in all places and partake of the fruit that is delicious above all others. If you take upon yourself his yolk, it will be light.

22.

MISSIONARY WORK, CONTINUED

Elder Warren M. Crane had served a faithful mission in Georgia and Florida, but during his last month, on December 7, 1941, he realized he would be continuing on with a different kind of mission. Three days after his Utah homecoming he enlisted in the Air Force.

As a young airman he was assigned to Transport Command and occasionally passed through Pensacola, Florida, where he met with LDS church members and other military personnel. One Fast Sunday, after many testimonies were shared, a major walked to the front of the group and said, "I am not a member of your church, but I must tell you of an experience I had recently in North Africa. I'm a doctor on leave and just a short time ago I was working on a young man who had been mortally wounded. I was sure he would soon die, but he insisted on having two Mormons bless him.

"My assistant said there was one in the lab, so we called for him. When he arrived, the lab technician insisted on having a second Mormon assist him. The only one they could find was a German prisoner of war working nearby. He was brought to the hospital, and the two pulled the curtains around my dying patient. I don't know what they did, but when the curtains opened, something miraculous had happened. This wounded soldier seemed stronger, and from that moment began to recover and is alive today. I don't know what they had or did or what you have that I don't have, but I want it. I want what you have."

During a Sunday service Warren kept looking over at the woman playing the piano and kept trying to remember where he had seen her before. After the meeting, he approached her and said, "I know you." This woman seemed to recognize him and helped him remember by describing a cottage beside a large home that she lived in. Many wealthy people would not receive the missionaries so they would call on the domestic help living in what some may call servants' quarters. As she gave the date, address, and description, Warren remembered how he and his missionary companion had walked around back and knocked on her door. On that hot afternoon, she had answered the door with nothing on but her underwear. He smiled as he explained that he was so distracted that, "I just lowered my eyes and handed you a Book of Mormon and asked you to read it." She accepted it, read it, and was baptized. She laughed and said, "Yes, I am the one who answered the door in my underwear. Thank you for finding me."

As World War II continued, Warren and his good friend Lewis Merrill had befriended another younger Latter-day Saint named Boyd Packer who was struggling to make it through flight training. Such service and teaching to other members of the church is every bit as important as doing the same for those who have not yet found or accepted the Gospel. Because of childhood health problems, it was difficult for Boyd to complete his training. Both Warren and Lewis did everything they could to help.

During a practice session, Boyd tried some unique flying maneuvers and got into trouble. His plane began to spiral out of control and fall to the earth. Miraculously, he was able to pull it out of this "death spin." Realizing the danger he had been in, it was hard for him to sleep that night. Very late, he got out of bed and went out on the balcony to get some fresh air. Concerned that all was well, Warren got out of his bunk and went out to talk. Boyd confessed that he had almost gotten himself killed that day. "Didn't your trainer tell you how to get out of that spin?" asked Warren. "No, he never told me," was the reply. Comforting words of encouragement and assurance helped to change the perspective of the event. It helped to change the fear in the heart of a young man into the mature faith and gratitude of a future apostle.

Serving other members of the church is as much a part of missionary work as finding someone new to teach.

23.

MORAL PURITY

Brothers and sisters, I testify that Jesus Christ, under the direction of Heavenly Father, created this earth and placed all living things on it for the benefit of mankind. I testify that in our pre-earth life we all received the opportunity to gain a mortal body and be tested according to our faith and obedience. Our body is a temple of God. It is created in his image and is capable of participating with God in creating the bodies for his other children. It can and will be resurrected and glorified.

It may not be so important how large or small body is, but how we learn to control it, how we take care of it, and what we do with it that really matters. Harming or abusing our body, or someone else's, is a very serious sin. Giving life or taking life from another person without God's permission are two of the most serious sins we know of. Next to murder, sexual sin is the most serious. I testify that God's prophets have taught this throughout all the history of mankind. I add my testimony to theirs.

Evolution

In my sophomore and junior years of high school I took Zoology, Physiology, and Genetics from my teacher at my high school in Blackfoot, Idaho. Quite a few parents were upset because the teacher was introducing us to Darwin's Theory of Evolution and the survival of the fittest. He stimulated thinking that caused his students to question the very existence of God. Many liked what they heard and began to question everything.

I don't claim to know how God put all living things on the earth, but I testify that He did it, and we are here. Instead of evolving from slime to fish and then from monkeys to men and the survival of the fittest, I prefer to contemplate the Law of Eternal Progression and the survival of the most righteous. We have progressed from eternal intelligence to spirit children, then to mortal man, one day to be resurrected and glorified with the possibility of becoming like God himself. We can imagine ourselves as we think of the Savior's birth, mortal life, death, and resurrection. He has made the journey and we can follow in his footsteps.

Sexuality

We understand that there is a time and a season for everything. We know that before the marriage ordinance is performed it is unlawful and sinful to share sexual intimacy. After the marriage ordinance, it becomes a commandment. It is right and good and is ordained of God. After marriage we must be valiant to our spouse and not have improper sexual relations with any other person. Complete modesty should be exercised with all other individuals.

Parents, teach your children. Do not think that your 6 year olds do not know about "the facts of life." To this day, I can clearly remember just before school started, standing under the apple tree in the playground listening to my friend Gary enthusiastically explaining how babies are made. I was well informed before my parents chose to explain things to me during junior high school.

In our family, we have always spoken candidly with our young children about sexuality and morality. As in the temple, we explain that there are sacred things that we only discuss as a family or alone with parents. Once the conversation is over we emphasize that they are not to discuss these things with their friends or among themselves. We know, of course, that they probably will.

Pornography, whether visual or imagined, fosters an unnatural obsession with sex. Right now today, there are books, magazines, newspapers, movies, television programs and the Internet in our homes that contain pornography. The question is, "What are we going to do about it?"

If you think this is a little too old fashioned or too conservative, be careful with such thinking.

If something is not good for a child's mind, it is not good for an adult's mind. Do not view or read material that you don't want your children to view or read! If you do this, the Lord promises you that you will be happy and safe rather than sorry.

Keep a happy, healthy attitude and body. Take only good things in. Eat only what is good for you when and in the amounts that you need, and always not what you want. Go to bed early and get up early so your mind and body can be invigorated. Repent if need be and the youthful outlook on life will return. Freshness and hope will fill your soul.

24.

PATRIARCHAL BLESSINGS

Meaning and Guidance

A patriarchal blessing can be a "Liahona of light" in our lives. Just as the Lord provided a Liahona to direct Lehi, that same Lord provides for us a rare and priceless gift. It will give direction to our lives point out the hazards in our journey, chart our course, and give safe passage to our heavenly home.

"Patriarchal blessings contemplate an inspired declaration of the lineage of the recipient, and when so motivated by the Spirit, a prophetic and inspired statement of the life's mission of the recipient, together with such promises, cautions, admonitions which would be helpful in fulfillment of that life's mission. It being understood that all promises are conditional on obedience to the Gospel of the Lord, whose servant the patriarch is." (First Presidency letter to stake presidents)

This blessing is a personal revelation meant to motivate, inspire, and encourage faithfulness. Your patriarchal blessing contains chapters out of your book of eternal possibilities. Just as life is eternal, so a patriarchal blessing is eternal. Those promises not fulfilled in this life may be fulfilled in the next.

Study your blessing. It is not to be tucked away, but is to be read and reread. It is to be loved. It is to be followed.

Marcel and Sibyl Dunn

Elder and Sister Dunn were called as couple missionaries to Peru with no prior knowledge of the Spanish language. They occasionally wondered why the Lord would call them to South America where they were seemingly so ineffective and unable to use their talents. However, they met a young man on the street and invited him into the chapel to hear the missionary discussions. He accepted the invitation. Their Spanish was such that they could only read the discussions from the manual. When the young man asked a question that they didn't understand, they would just smile and keep on reading. The young man was later baptized and prepared to go on a mission.

When the district president found out about the baptism, he asked, "How can they be baptizing; they don't even speak Spanish?" But this couple did a great job, and the people loved them. They were a great strength to the members just by being there.

After a time, Elder Dunn was called as a mission patriarch. He traveled all over the mission giving Patriarchal Blessings. In the last five months of his mission he gave 695 beautiful Patriarchal Blessings. The first one was in English, but the rest were in Spanish! He signed the last three blessings just before he got on the airplane to return to the United States. What a great blessing to Peru!

25.

PEACE THROUGH ADVERSITY

The American Dream

The "American Dream" inspires all to be free, to be your best, to prosper and accomplish great things, and be the kind of person that you are destined to become. Most people are willing to make great sacrifices, and are willing to do almost anything to achieve their goals and realize these dreams. For example, in sports, we all want to get into the game, excel, show our stuff, and win. We all want to survive and live a full life. We all want to be loved, to feel important, and to enjoy a wide variety of the beauties of life.

Our Mortal Dream

In our pre-earth life, we also had a dream, a "Mortal Dream." This dream was inspired by our Heavenly Father's Plan to come to earth and gain a body and to be tested to see whether we would choose between good or evil. Part of the testing process was to help us grow and develop the attributes of godliness so we could become like him. Everyone who has ever been born was willing and probably very excited to come to earth, no matter what the circumstances, no matter what the challenges. It was so important that we were willing to accept almost anything to achieve that goal.

As we were born, a veil of forgetfulness was drawn across our minds, and we forgot what we knew before. We started to make our way in the highways of life, to fight our way up, and to become worthy citizens. Sometimes loving parents, teachers, or friends helped us. Sometimes we were left alone to make our way. Sometimes, this is as it should be.

Life was intended to deal us some heavy blows and to offer us some real challenges. This was part of the plan to help us realize our "Mortal Dream" and someday return to live with God. He has taught us through his prophets that gratitude is a key to finding peace.

Gratitude

The importance of a grateful heart is taught in this hymn:

Count Your Blessings
(Hymns of the Church of Jesus Christ of Latter-day Saints, 241)

When upon life's billows you are tempest tossed,
When you are discouraged, thinking all is lost,
Count your many blessings; name them one by one,
And it will surprise you what the Lord has done.

Are you ever burdened with a load of care?
Does the cross seem heavy you are called to bear?
Count your many blessings; every doubt will fly,
And you will be singing as the days go by.

When you look at others with their lands and gold,
Think that Christ has promised you his wealth untold.
Count your many blessings; money cannot buy
Your reward in heaven nor your home on high.

So amid the conflict, whether great or small,
Do not be discouraged; God is over all.
Count your many blessings; angels will attend,
Help and comfort give you to your journey's end.

Chorus:
Count your blessings, name them one by one.
Count your many blessings, see what God has done.

Discouragement

The trials and tribulations of life can discourage the strongest Latter-day Saint. Some are asking the question, "Why am I not happy?" They wonder "If I keep the commandments, why am I not happy?" Have you ever had that feeling, or asked yourself those questions, or heard someone expressing these feelings? Have you struggled to find peace through overcoming adversity?

The Robe

One evening I watched a special movie with my children. It was called *The Robe*. I had seen the movie as a child, and it had impressed me then as it did that night. In one scene, Richard Burton, an avenging and bitter Roman soldier, was speaking to a young crippled woman who had been bitter and unhappy until Jesus healed her soul. The soldier demanded to know why Jesus hadn't healed her body if he had healed so many others. Her answer was powerful. She said, "Oh, he could have healed me all right, but he let me stay the way I am so others like me could know they could be happy too."

The Winds of Life

A long time ago, my father and I visited my older brother and his family, who were living just north of Perth in Australia. His company had sent him there on a special project. He showed us a very interesting kind of tree along the coast near the town of Greennough. The trees were all bent way over, and the branches touched the ground. The prevailing winds blowing inland from the ocean had gradually caused these trees to bend over. My brother wrote the following poem, which helps us relate this natural phenomenon to our own lives:

Oh winds of Greennough by the sea,
Your constant force distorts the tree.
Oh winds of life, though strong you be,
I will not bend an inch for three.

While life's forces are truly challenging, the winds of life and the adversities we face are exactly what we need to grow.

Opposition Needed

We understand that it is necessary to experience opposition in order to become strong. In I Nephi 2:11 we read, "For it must needs be, that there is an opposition in all things." This hymn teaches us this lesson.

God Moves in a Mysterious Way
(Hymns of the Church of Jesus Christ of Latter-day Saints, 285)

God moves in a mysterious way
His wonders to perform;
He plants his footsteps in the sea
And rides upon the storm.

Ye fearful Saints, fresh courage take;
The clouds ye so much dread
Are big with mercy and shall break
In blessings on your head.

His purposes will ripen fast,
Unfolding every hour;
The bud may have a bitter taste,
But sweet will be the flower.

Blind unbelief is sure to err
And scan his works in vain;

God is his own interpreter,
And he will make it plain.

With a thankful heart, and a yearning soul, we can know the reasons for, and the rewards of, overcoming adversity. We can recognize the lessons to learn from our trials. If it is not obvious, we can seek the Lord's help. We have the invitation, "Ask and ye shall receive, seek and ye shall find, knock and it shall be open unto you" (Matthew 7:7). What the Lord reveals to us, we can know, understand and accept. What he doesn't reveal to us, we can trust that He will help us to use our trials to our own advantage and development.

For many years we have experienced opposition against the Church of Jesus Christ of Latter-day Saints. The spirit of criticism and contention is not of the Lord. It is the spirit of Satan who wishes to destroy God's Kingdom.

We also understand that all people have their own agency to choose the good from the evil in all things. We choose how we respond to adversity. Some people want to change the church by criticizing its members, its leaders or doctrines. We understand the importance of modern-day revelation in guiding us through these last days of trials and tribulation. We can be assured that the Gospel will go forth and the truth shall prevail.

I am convinced that the opposition we now face will be something that will help us prepare for greater opposition in the future. We can look at this opposition as a great opportunity for the missionaries to work more closely with members as they prepare people for baptism. We can meet this opposition with a cheerful smile and an invitation for people to open their hearts and hear our message and then judge for themselves if we preach the truth or if we are trying to deceive them.

As a member of the church, each man has the opportunity to receive the priesthood and to serve others. Each woman covenants to take upon herself the burdens of others and learns to lift and inspire through service.

Individually, we all have trials, tribulations and varying degrees of adversity. Some of it is self-inflicted, some of it is intentionally inflicted upon us by others, and some of it is just part of this temporal life. We are admonished to expect it, be prepared for it and to receive it as cheerfully as possible. Such experience is one of the reasons for our coming into mortality. It has been said that, "Man is not an earthly being having a spiritual experience, but a spiritual being having an earthly experience."

Apostle Paul

The Apostle Paul gives us great encouragement in his words found in 2 Corinthians 7:4: "I am filled with comfort, I am exceeding joyful in all our tribulation." Then, after listing all the various perils he had passed through, which included being beaten, stoned, shipwrecked, robbed, left hungry, cold and naked, he concluded by saying, "If I must need glory, I will glory of the things which concern mine infirmities."

In 2 Corinthians 11, Paul said that he pleaded with the Lord regarding his weaknesses, and the Lord said, "My grace is sufficient for thee: for my strength is made perfect in weakness. Most gladly therefore will I glory in my infirmities, that the power of Christ may rest upon me. Therefore I take pleasure in infirmities, in reproaches, in necessities, in persecutions, in distresses for Christ's sake: for when I am weak, then am I strong."

Joseph Smith

The Prophet Joseph Smith was also strengthened through overcoming adversity. As a child, Joseph had suffered with the usual illnesses, but especially with an infected leg. He had to have it operated on without anesthetic. The leg was lame, and he walked with crutches for several years. Joseph was tempered by hard work on the family farm. As a teenager, he was persecuted by angry ministers.

While Joseph was in the Liberty Jail and had been pleading with the Lord because of the cold, horrible living conditions and resulting great suffering there, God taught him a beautiful lesson: "My son, peace be unto thy soul; thine adversity and thine afflictions shall be but a small moment; and then, if thou endure it well, God shall exalt thee on high; thou shalt triumph over all thy foe" (D&C 121:7-8).

Later on, being very familiar with adversity, Joseph describes his feelings in D&C 127:2. He said, "And as for the perils which I am called to pass through, they seem but a small thing to me, as the wrath of man has been my common lot all the days of my life; and for what cause it seems mysterious, unless I was ordained from before the foundation of the world for some good end, or bad, as you may choose to call it. Judge ye for yourselves. God knoweth all these things, whether it be good or bad. But nevertheless, deep water is what I am want to swim in. It all has become a second nature to me; and I feel, like Paul, to glory in tribulation; for this day has the God of my fathers delivered me out of them all, and will deliver me from henceforth; for behold, and lo, I shall triumph over all my enemies, for the Lord God hath spoken it."

Neal A. Maxwell

Elder Neal A. Maxwell quoted Malcum Muggerage, a modern day philosopher, who said, "All the happenings in this world, including the most terrible disasters and sufferings will be seen in eternity as in some mysterious way a blessing, as part of God's love . . . otherwise our mortal existence is no more than a night in a second class motel." Elder Maxwell explains that what Mr. Muggerage was saying is that we are going to have to have some first-class challenges in our life if we are to have a **first class experience**. Prepare your family for hard times, for trials and suffering.

Elder Maxwell points out that there are three types of adversity: 1) Suffering because of sin; 2) suffering built into the fabric of life; and 3) suffering to test us. We can expect it. We may be able to minimize it by preparation, attitude and obedience, but it will come.

Lawrence Higginson

My friend Lawrence Higginson shared this thought about adversity: "Suffering is a blessing in disguise. The experience of going through pain and anguish enables us to understand and empathize with what others have gone through. We need to realize that we should worry about *what life expects of us* and not *what we expect of life*. All great people throughout history have gone through pain and anguish of spirit and body sometime during their lives. Blessings come after tribulation. Joy comes after sorrow and strife if we learn to endure it well. These tribulations have a refining effect. Our spirits are brought closer to the Lord as we exercise faith and trust in him. Know that what we go through is for our best good. Approach life with full purpose of heart, and rejoice in the experiences of life, great and small."

Be of Good Cheer

Let us take heart and be of good cheer. God is with us. When we feel overwhelmed with adversity or discouragement let us "count our blessings" and look for the meaning of that adversity and how it will help us to attain the attributes of Godliness.

Be thankful that you are counted worthy to have a burden to bear. Be very thankful that you can bear one another's burdens. And be ever so thankful that Jesus Christ bears all of our sins and burdens if we let him. He said:

"Come unto me, all ye that labor and are heavy laden, and I will give you rest. Take my yoke upon you, and learn of me; for I am meek and lowly in heart: and ye shall find rest unto your souls. For my yoke is easy, and my burden is light" (Matthew 11:28-30).

God Loves Us Personally

God loves each of us. He wants us to grow. Therefore He will allow us to experience adversity. But He will help us overcome it. This is his promise, "Peace I leave with you, my peace I give unto you: not as the world giveth, give I unto you. Let not your heart be troubled, neither let it be afraid" (John 14:27).

We also receive peace and comfort in the words of this beautiful hymn:

Though Deepening Trials

(Hymns of the Church of Jesus Christ of Latter-day Saints, 122)

Though deepening trials throng your way
Press on; press on, ye Saints of God!
Ere long the resurrection day
Will spread its life and truth abound,

Though out-ward ills await us here,
The time, at longest, is not long
Ere Jesus Christ will reappear,
Surrounded by a glorious throng,

Lift up your hearts in praise to God;
Let your rejoicings never cease.

Though tribulations rage abroad,
Christ says, "In me ye shall have peace."

What though our rights have been assailed?
What though by foes we've been despoiled?
Jehovah's promise has not failed;
Jehovah's purpose is not foiled.

This work is moving on apace,
And great events are rolling forth;
The kingdom of the latter days,
The "little stone" must fill the earth.

Though Satan rage, 'tis all in vain;
The words the ancient prophet spoke
Sure as the throne of God remains;
Nor men nor devils can revoke.

All glory to his holy name
Who sends his faithful servants forth
To prove the nations, to proclaim
Salvation's tidings through the earth.

26.

PERFECTION

In a conference of missionaries, Sister Christensen shared her conversion and stated that during her first months of investigating the church, she thought that Mormons were perfect. She also said that she thought I was perfect. Before her baptism she felt inadequate to live up to what was expected of a Latter-day Saint. I felt inadequate to live up to her expectations, and tried to convince her that I was *not* perfect.

How can we keep the commandment, "Be ye therefore perfect, even as your Father in Heaven is perfect" (Matt. 5:48). I believe there are three approaches to obeying that commandment. One, we can be exact, or perfect, in doing a certain thing. Two, we can be without sin. Three, we can develop all of our Godly attributes.

At first, our efforts and progress seems small and temporarily short lived, but nevertheless, we are progressing and moving forward. Remembering and doing the following may help us in this progress:

- Perfection is our goal.
- Because we are not perfect does not mean we are failing.
- Everyone has felt feelings of failure.
- We need to have realistic expectations of our progress.
- We must move forward in spite of our weaknesses, feelings of failure, or mistakes.
- We are judged by both our works and the desires of our heart.
- Endure to the end!

27.

PRAYER

Years ago an old lady down south had no money to buy food. But with complete trust in God, she got down on her knees and prayed aloud, "Dear Lord, please send me a side of bacon and a sack of corn meal." Over and over again, the old lady repeated the same plea in a loud voice. One of the town's worst characters, over hearing her supplication, decided to play a trick on her. Hurrying to the nearest store, he bought a side of bacon and a sack of corn meal. Upon his return to the cabin, he dropped the food down the chimney. It landed right in front of the hungry woman as she knelt in prayer.

Jumping to her feet, she exclaimed jubilantly: "Oh, Lord, you've answered my prayer!" Then she ran all around the neighborhood telling everyone the good news. This was too much for the scoundrel. He ridiculed her before the others by telling how he had dropped the food down the chimney himself. The wise old woman quickly replied: "Well, the Devil may have brought it, but it was the Lord who sent it."

Bruce R. McConkie stated: "To pray is to speak with God, either vocally or by forming the thoughts involved in the mind. Prayers may properly include expressions of praise, thanksgiving, and admiration; they are the solemn occasions during which the children of God petition their eternal Father for those things, both temporal and spiritual, which they feel are needed to sustain them in all the varied tests of this mortal probation. Prayers are occasions of confession—occasions when in humility and contrition, having broken hearts and contrite spirits, the saints confess their sins to Deity and implore him to grant his cleansing forgiveness."

Spencer W. Kimball wrote: "We pray for enlightenment, then go with all our might and our books and our thoughts and righteousness to get the inspiration. We ask for judgment, then use all our powers to act wisely and develop wisdom. We pray for success in our work and then study hard and strive with all our might to help answer our prayers. When we pray for health we must live the laws of health and do all in our power to keep our bodies well and vigorous. We pray for protection and then take reasonable precaution to avoid danger. There must be works with faith. How foolish it would be to ask the Lord to give us knowledge, but how wise to ask the Lord's help to acquire knowledge, to study constructively, to think clearly, and to retain things that we have learned. How stupid to ask the Lord to protect us if we unnecessarily drive at excessive speeds or try foolish stunts."

God answers prayers in many ways, by a calm feeling, coincidences, dreams, impressions, signs, opening doors, recurrence of certain themes, assistance, faith, feelings of peace, burning of the heart, whispering by the still small voice, verbal communication, through others. He also answers prayers through stupor of thought or closed doors.

Be patient. See if you have experienced any of the ways God answers prayers. Once you realize that there are many ways answers can come, you may not feel so deprived. Don't force it by trying too hard. If the feeling comes, it will come in a most natural, easy way. Continue to pray as a believer.

The most significant prayer in LDS Church history is when the young Joseph Smith received an answer to his prayer in the grove of trees in Palmyra, New York. He cried unto God to know which church was true, and was rewarded with a vision of God the Father and the Son. He saw them. He heard the voice of God. He was told that his sins had been forgiven. He was given instructions to join none of the churches of the day. It was a powerful answer to a prayer that changed everything for him and his family, and for us.

William McKinley and the Philippines

At the end of the Spanish-American War in 1898, the Philippines were taken from Spanish rule and awarded to the United States. In an interview with U.S. President William McKinley, he stated: "I have been criticized a good deal about the Philippines, but I don't deserve it. The truth is. I didn't want the Philippines, and when they came to us, as a gift from the gods, I did not know what to do with them. . . . I sought counsel from all sides—Democrats as well as Republicans—but got little help. . . . I walked the floor of the White House night after night until midnight; and I am not ashamed to tell you, gentlemen, that I went down on my knees and prayed to Almighty God for light and guidance more than one night.

"And one night late it came to me this way: 1) That we could not give them back to Spain—that would be cowardly and dishonorable; 2) that we could not turn them over to France or Germany—that would be bad business and discreditable; 3) that we could not leave them to themselves—they were unfit for self-government, and they would soon have anarchy and misrule over there worse than Spain's was; and 4) that there was nothing left for us to do but to take them all, and to educate the people, and uplift and . . . Christianize them, and, by God's grace, do the very best we could by them, as our fellowmen for whom Christ also died . . ."

What If God Had Voice Mail?

We have learned to live with voice mail as a necessary part of modern life. What if God decided to install voice mail? Imagine praying and hearing this:

> Thank you for calling The Lord's House. Please select from the following options:

- Press 1 for GENERAL REQUESTS.
- Press 2 for THANKSGIVING.
- Press 3 for COMPLAINTS.
- Press 4 for HEALING.
- Press 5 for HELP WITH THE IRS.
- Press 6 for RAIN or No RAIN.
- Press 7 for MIRACLES.
- Press 8 for LOTTERY WINNING NUMBERS.
- Press 9 for ALL OTHER INQUIRIES OR JUST TO SAY "HI"
- Press 0 to hear this menu again.

What if God used the familiar excuse: "I'm sorry, all the angels are helping other sinners right now. Please stay on the line. Your call is important to us and will be answered in this millennium.

Another version of Heavenly Voice Mail might sound like this:

- If you would like to speak to Gabriel, press 11.
- For Michael, press 22.
- For a directory of the other Archangels, press 33.
- If you would like to hear King David sing a Psalm while you are holding, please press 55. Then wait for the beep and enter the number of the Psalm you wish to hear.

- To find out if a loved one has been assigned to heaven, press 62. Enter his or her social security number, then press the pound key.
- For answers to nagging questions about dinosaurs, the age of the earth, where Noah's ark is, Darwin, Hitler, the Pope, and UFOs, please wait until you arrive here, as answers can only be understood from a "heavenly perspective."
- To reach Lucifer, press 666, and your call will be automatically transferred. Please be careful, as your receiver may become warm.
- For emergencies, refer to your Bible.

28.

PURPOSE OF LIFE

God is our loving Heavenly Father. Jesus Christ is his son, and we are also his sons and daughters. God has a plan of happiness for us to progress and to become like him.

Our life before we were born on this earth is called our pre-mortal existence. In this pre-earth life, we lived in the presence of our Heavenly Father as his spirit children. He has a glorified body of flesh and bones, but we only had a spirit body.

During our pre-mortal existence, everyone who has been born on the earth chose to follow God's plan, which was presented to us by our brother and Savior, Jesus Christ. This plan includes gaining a body and learning to use our agency to choose good over evil. Those who *rejected* this plan rebelled and followed Lucifer, (the Devil, or Satan), and were cast out of Father's presence and were denied a physical body.

Birth is when our spirit receives a mortal body so we can live on the earth. Here we learn to follow commandments and eternal laws. We gain intelligence. We get experience. We usually marry and have children to nurture and teach. Here we develop faith. However, we cannot progress without opposition. Life is a struggle to choose good or evil. Satan now dwells upon the earth and continues to influence us and tempt us to follow him. Sometimes we give in to temptations and suffer the consequences. No one is perfect, and everyone makes mistakes. Our Savior, Jesus Christ, atoned for these mistakes and made it possible for us to continue to progress in spite of our sins.

Our earth life is but a small part of our eternal existence. Physical death comes to all. It is the separation of the spirit from the mortal body. The spirit world is where our spirits go between death and resurrection. Paradise is that part of the spirit world in which the righteous spirits who have departed from this life await the resurrection of the body.

The resurrection is the reuniting of the spirit with the body in an immortal state, no longer subject to disease or death. Because of the atonement and resurrection of Jesus Christ, all humankind, no matter how righteous or unrighteous on earth, will be resurrected and redeemed from physical death. After we are resurrected, we will stand before the Lord to be judged according to our desires and actions. Each of us will accordingly receive an eternal dwelling place in a specific kingdom of glory. The Lord taught this principle when He said, "In my Father's house are many mansions" (John 14:2). We have the opportunity to progress as far as we desire. We are the one who decides our destiny.

29.

RICHES AND RIGHTEOUSNESS

The Formula for Prosperity

In Malachi 3:9 we read about the curse upon the land and its people. We can be assured that the Lord has given us specific laws that govern prosperity and has taught us how we can revive the blessings that come from obedience to God's commandments.

In a recent newspaper article, the Church of Jesus Christ of Latter-day Saints was accused of being a "religion that has money as its God." The article quoted Alma 1:31 that says, "And thus they did prosper and become far more wealthy than those who did not belong to their church."

The article also quoted from 4 Nephi 1:23 which states, "That the people had multiplied, insomuch that they were spread upon all the face of the land, and that they had become exceedingly rich, because of their prosperity in Christ."

You must understand that riches are not our most important goal, but they seem to sometimes be a by-product of obedience. Financial prosperity can also assist the building up of the Kingdom of God here on the earth. To avoid any misunderstanding about this, let us consider doing the following:

1. Establish a clear understanding of the importance of developing spiritually first, and temporally second.
2. Review God's promises to those who live in this land and to all who obey him.
3. Outline the fundamental laws of wealth and prosperity.

Priorities

We are counseled to have our priorities in order. We are warned in 3 Nephi 13:19-24 not to love money more than God; ". . . for where your treasure is there will your heart be also. No man can serve two masters; for either he will hate the one and love the other, or else he will hold to the one and despise the other. Ye cannot serve God and Mammon."

No Virtue in Poverty

There is no virtue in being poor. God has not created you to be poor or to be under a curse. He wants us to prosper, but more importantly, He wants us to rely upon him and obey him. We need only to ask of him and then do our part.

We can and must desire to prosper! "Where there's a will, there's a way." It is easier to prosper than to remain poor. We are exhorted by Amulek in Alma 34:17-19 to pray over all of our spiritual and temporal affairs. "Pray over all your household, the crops of your fields, for your flocks, for your welfare, and for the welfare of those who are around you, that ye may prosper in them" and "that they may increase."

Laws of Wealth

Now we might ask, "What are the Laws of Wealth?" They are true and simple, but then the truth is always simple. They are as follows:

1. Pay an honest tithe and give generous offerings (see Malachi 3:6-12).
2. Budget and control expenditures. Do not spend more than you earn. Avoid debt.
3. A part of all we earn is ours to keep. Pay at least a tenth of your income to yourself, to be used for savings and sound

investments. Money saved is like a slave working to help you prosper. Wealth, like a tree, grows from a small seed.

4. Increase your ability to earn through additional education and work experience.
5. Insure against tragedy or death. It is wise to have adequate health and life insurance. You cannot afford to be without protection.
6. You also need the "assurance" of a supply of food, clothing, fuel, medicines, money, etc.
7. Assure an income for the future by investing wisely. It is always better to take a little precaution than to have a great regret afterwards. Counsel with wise people, and take advice only from those who know. It is a good idea to make your home a profitable investment.
8. Take advantage of opportunity, and do not procrastinate. Opportunity waits for no man or woman. However, good luck waits and comes to that person who accepts opportunity. We can be our worst enemy if we are not prepared, or if we are afraid.
9. To prosper a little you need only to work hard for your employer. To prosper a lot you need to be your own employer.
10. Have faith, be honest, work hard, and work smart.

It's easier to become wealthy than to endure poverty. Every person has the same amount of time in a day or in a year. It is what we do with it that makes all the difference. The same thing applies to money. Desire, discipline and effort will determine the amount of your wealth and satisfaction regarding your efforts.

Control Expenses

Expenses will always grow to meet our income unless we control them. Our wants are always bigger than our means.

Decide what a *necessary* expense is, and what a *discretionary* expense is. Remember that weeds steal water and nourishment from your growing tree. Make sure you carefully study your spending and living habits, make a category for each expense, select those that are necessary, and eliminate the rest. By developing a budget plan and living within its guidelines you can see clearly how to manage your money and prosper.

Avoid Debt

Avoid debt like the plague. Borrow only for wise purposes or business opportunities. Education and home ownership are among the few acceptable long-term debts. If you do have debts, pay them promptly to retain your self-respect and reputation. If possible, it is wise to make double principle payments to pay debts off in less than half the time. Never keep high-interest credit card debt. If you already have it, throw all your resources into paying it off.

Invest in the Future

Wealth, like a giant Sequoia tree, grows from a tiny seed. The sooner you plant it the sooner it will begin to grow. Now is the time to appropriately invest your savings. Care and attention will insure that the tree will not wither up and die. Seek expert counsel from wise men who are experts in their field of investments. Carefully measure your risk and your desired return. Invest wisely, with great caution, and don't be tempted to try to "get rich quick."

But, don't try to save too much too fast. Smell the roses along the way and enjoy life to fullest. There are many things other than money that also merit and require one's time and effort. It is important to remember that the money we spend today gives us only the things of the moment, but the money we save and invest will grow and provide additional income in the future.

The Promise

What is the promise? The promise is the same to us as it was to the ancient inhabitants of the Americas. In Alma 50:20 the Lord said, "Blessed art thou and thy children; and they shall be blessed, inasmuch as they shall keep my commandments they shall prosper in the land. But remember, inasmuch as they will not keep my commandments they shall be cut off from the presence of the Lord."

We must know and believe that we and our nation will prosper! The prosperity of any nation depends on the prosperity of its individual citizens. With this wealth we will do great things. Wealth is power, and with this power many things are possible.

30.

SERVICE

Service is contagious, and it changes the world. It begins by changing us! When I think about this, I think about Jennie Dudley feeding the homeless in Salt Lake City. The following newspaper article written by Lois M. Collins was printed in the *Deseret News*:

They come by the hundreds on Sunday morning, down on their luck and hungry -- many of them without homes, some without hope.

Jennie Dudley feeds them under the viaduct near Pioneer Park on Fourth South. Nearly a hundred Sundays have come and gone since she began, but her basic equipment is unchanged: camp stoves and faith that God, through caring individuals, will provide food.

She never knows in advance what they'll be eating, or who will help her cook and clean up. Until the food arrives, she can't begin to guess how many hungry people will gather. "When there's a lot of food, I know we can expect lots of people. Somehow, praise God, there is always enough."

She began in a small way, with a camp stove, a coffee pot, a little coffee, a ball of fry bread, an iron skillet and a little honey and butter. Hers was a solo act -- for a few minutes. But someone drove by, asked what she was doing and returned with food. It has worked that way ever since. "I don't try to organize things in advance," she said. "It's always provided, and it's never all fruit or all eggs or all meat. It's always a complete meal." Some weeks, she and other volunteers serve 600 or 700 people.

31.

SPEECH AND LANGUAGE

"If you're going to talk the talk, then you've gotta walk the walk!"

Before we get started with walking, listen to what has been said about the talkin'. There has been a lot of study done about the origin of language and application of linguistics.

Since the founding of our country, our society has undergone dramatic changes in verbal communication. Technology, travel, and culture have had a lot to do with it. Much has been good, but there is still a lot left to be desired.

Language of Faith

In the beginning, "The whole earth was of one language, and one speech" (Genesis 11:1). Adam and Eve taught their children to read and write. "And by them their children were taught to read and write, having a language which was pure and undefiled" (Pearl of Great Price; Moses 6:6).

Their language was pure and undefiled and was an expression of power. We see an example in Enoch: "And so great was the faith of Enoch that he led the people of God, and their enemies came to battle against them; and he spake the word of the Lord, and the earth trembled, and the mountains fled, even according to his command; and the rivers of water were turned out of their course; and the roar of the lions was heard out of the wilderness; and all nations feared greatly, so powerful was the word of Enoch, and so great was the power of the language which God had given him" (Moses 7:17).

Others used this language to do evil, and God destroyed them in the flood. After the flood, they built a great tower. The Lord was not pleased:

"And the LORD came down to see the city and the tower, which the children of men builded. And the LORD said, Behold, the people are one, and they have all one language; and this they begin to do: and now nothing will be restrained from them, which they have imagined to do. Go to, let us go down, and there confound their language, that they may not understand one another's speech.

"So the LORD scattered them abroad from thence upon the face of all the earth: and they left off to build the city. Therefore is the name of it called Babel; because the LORD did there confound the language of all the earth: and from thence did the LORD scatter them abroad upon the face of all the earth" (Genesis 11:5-9).

Today, we live in a world of confusion and pollution. All the languages of the earth are degenerate forms of expression and communication. Few people are able to clearly articulate the word of God. The Lord has promised a better day when he said:

"Therefore wait ye upon me, saith the LORD, until the day that I rise up to the prey: for my determination [is] to gather the nations, that I may assemble the kingdoms, to pour upon them mine indignation, [even] all my fierce anger: for all the earth shall be devoured with the fire of my jealousy.

"For then will I turn to the people a pure language, that they may all call upon the name of the LORD, to serve him with one consent" (Zephaniah 3:8-9).

Many people, including the prophets of scripture, have commented on the power of language as spoken or written, and the influence of the Holy Ghost. Nephi said:

"Do ye not remember that I said unto you that after ye had received the Holy Ghost ye could speak with the tongue of angels? And now, how Angels speak by the power of the Holy Ghost; wherefore, they speak the words of Christ. Wherefore, I said unto you, feast upon the words of Christ; for behold, the words of Christ will tell you all things what ye should do. Wherefore, now after I have spoken these words, if ye cannot understand them it will be because ye ask not, neither do ye knock; wherefore, ye are not brought into the light, but must perish in the dark" (2 Nephi 32:2-4).

And

"And now I, Nephi, cannot write all the things which were taught among my people; neither am I mighty in writing, like unto speaking; for when a man speaketh by the power of the Holy Ghost the power of the Holy Ghost carrieth it unto the hearts of the children of men" (2 Nephi 33:1).

Ether also pleaded with the Lord:

"And I said unto him: Lord, the Gentiles will mock at these things, because of our weakness in writing; for Lord thou hast made us mighty in word by faith, but thou hast not made us mighty in writing; for thou hast made all this people that they could speak much, because of the Holy Ghost which thou hast given them;

"And thou hast made us that we could write but little, because of the awkwardness of our hands. Behold, thou hast not made us mighty in writing like unto the brother of Jared, for thou madest him that the things which he wrote were mighty even as thou art, unto the overpowering of man to read them.

"Thou hast also made our words powerful and great, even that we cannot write them; wherefore, when we write we behold our weakness, and stumble because of the placing of our words; and I fear lest the Gentiles shall mock at our words" (Ether 12:23-25).

When the Mulekites were discovered by the people of Mosiah, it was noted that one of their great weaknesses was in their language and lack of records. We read:

"And at the time that Mosiah discovered them, they had become exceedingly numerous. Nevertheless, they had had many wars and serious contentions, and had fallen by the sword from time to time; and their language had become corrupted; and they had brought no records with them; and they denied the being of their Creator; and Mosiah, nor the people of Mosiah, could understand them.

"But it came to pass that Mosiah caused that they should be taught in his language. And it came to pass that after they were taught in the language of Mosiah, Zarahemla gave a genealogy of his fathers, according to his memory; and they are written, but not in these plates" (Omni 1:17-18).

Even in missionary work, the teaching of a "new language" is important, as related in 2 Nephi 32:2-4, and evidenced by Alma and the sons of Mosiah teaching the Lamanites their purer and written language along with the Gospel.

The Book of Mormon prophets acknowledge their weaknesses in writing. Nephi even admits that there are expressions that cannot be written.

"And then I do make a record of the things which I have seen with mine own eyes. And I know the record which I make to be a just and a true record; nevertheless there are many things which, according to our language, we are not able to write" (3 Nephi 5:17-18).

And:

"And it came to pass that he went again a little way off and prayed unto the Father; And tongue cannot speak the words which he prayed, neither can be written by man the words which he prayed. And the multitude did hear and do bear record; and their hearts were open and they did understand in their hearts the words which he prayed. Nevertheless, so great and marvelous were the words which he prayed that they cannot be written, neither can they be uttered by man" (3 Nephi 19:31-34).

Thus we see that there can be beautiful and dramatic results from studying and speaking the Lord's word.

32.

STANDARDS, LAWS, AND THE GOLDEN RULE

Man-Made Standards

The world has many standards of weights and measures, distance and speed. There are standards for educational excellence, for movie and entertainment content, and for fashion. Sports standards are clearly defined by rules, penalties and records. Language standards are defined by grammar, accent and definition. These standards are all created by people who change them from time to time and place to place.

Eternal Standards and Laws

There are eternal standards, or laws, that do not change. They are fixed, and no matter what people do or decide to change, these eternal principles continue in force. When asked about the most important law, Jesus responded, "Thou shalt love the Lord thy God with all thy heart, and with all thy soul and with all thy mind. This is the first and great commandment. And the second is like unto it, Thou shalt love thy neighbor as thyself."

The Golden Rule

Even people who don't believe in God recognize the Golden Rule as the best way to treat others. "Do unto others as you would have them do unto you" will never become obsolete.

33.

STRESS FITNESS

Life has purpose and meaning. It is our classroom to learn to reach our potential and become the great people we are destined to be. Regardless of whether or not we believe we actually signed up for this experience, we are here. Why not make the best of it? As the cartoon character Ziggy says, "It beats all the alternatives."

Understanding Stress

Stress is a normal part of life and helps us develop, grow and overcome. We experience stress at every age and stage of our life. It is a normal physical and emotional response to the changes and challenges in our life. Without it, we would never learn, overcome, or achieve. However, if we have too much for too long, it can cause problems. Most stress is experienced when dealing with change and opposition. Thank goodness for both.

As children, we are experiencing a whole new world of sight, sound, speech, taste, touch and control. As teenagers, we become aware of learning, emotions, discipline, acceptance, self-esteem, dreams and disappointment. Then as young adults, we transition to being responsible, becoming educated, getting new jobs, developing relationships, and establishing goals and a family. Then during those years of providing, we look after others, make our contributions to society and share with others what we have experienced and learned. Finally, in old age, we struggle with the changes that come with retirement, aging, loss of health and wondering why others don't seem to get it.

Levels of Stress

For simplicity, let's divide stress into four levels. This will help us recognize, evaluate and deal with stress in a more effective and productive way. The levels will be called: 1) Good; 2) Uncomfortable; 3) Bad; and 4) Dangerous. Periodically assessing your stresses and levels of stress will help you maintain balance and use stress to the best of your advantage.

A *good stress* level would be when you are happy, confident and ready to meet challenges. You recover quickly from setbacks and your relationship with others is healthy. Keep up the good work.

An *uncomfortable stress* level is when you feel tense, worried or anxious, and you have trouble getting along with others. Don't be hard on yourself. Relax and read some uplifting or listen to inspiring music.

A *bad level* is evident when you are upset, emotionally exhausted, easily angered, and discouraged. Pray, search for solutions, and get help if this continues for more than three days.

The *dangerous level* requires immediate attention by seeking help. If possible, you should take a break from the stress causers and make sure you are properly nourishing your body, mind and spirit.

Kinds of Stress

General stress just comes with moving through life one day at a time. We will also experience physical stress depending on how much work or movement we do. It is also affected by our diet, our ability to rest sufficiently and the safety and health of the environment we are in.

Our *emotional stress* level is manifested in our thinking and emotions. We experience emotional distress depending on our self-esteem, relationships and level of required activities.

Social stress is definitely related to our interaction with new people and our relationship with those we know. On top of this, intellectual stress will be realized as we struggle to learn, teach, plan, manage expectations, adapt to change and understand life itself.

Finally, *spiritual stress* can be the most challenging because it comes with trying to understand the universe, our life, who we are, where we came from before we were born, and where we go after this life. Is there a God, and what is my relationship to all these other people in my house and on this earth?

There are valuable resources, principles and practices to help us take advantage of the good stress and to reduce or manage the bad stress. The most valuable are relaxation, prayer, scripture study, and the influence of the Holy Spirit. The best medicine for bad stress is work, uplifting activity, and helping others.

Response to Stress

Attitude is the most important element in how you respond to stress. Your perception of stress will determine how you process it and react to it. The results of your reactions will yield strengthening or debilitating results. Think positive thoughts and change negative thoughts into positive ones. Be aware that everyone is probably dealing with stress. Be a good listener, smile, say kind things to others, and help them along their way. You can make the world a better place by making people happy.

Prayer and journal keeping will give you strength and help you learn from stressful situations. If you acknowledge God in all things you will feel his spirit influencing you in many ways. The best antidote to relieve your pain is to help someone else with theirs. Music has magic in it. Sing a lot and listen to good music. Get plenty of exercise and rest. Eat well and don't take anything into your body or mind that is unhealthy. Manage your expectations, and focus on what needs to be done right now. Don't try to control others. Take regular breaks and don't get down on yourself. Be grateful, have faith and take one step at a time.

34.

TEMPLES FOR NOW AND ETERNITY

Temples and Revelation

We learn many valuable concepts from the old book, *Gems from the Teachings of the Prophets,* by John A. Widtsoe. The following gives insight into the sacred value of the temple and obtaining revelations:

"Revelation ... is not imposed upon a person; it must be drawn to us by faith, seeking and working. Just so to the man or woman *who goes through the temple*, with open eyes, heeding the symbols and the covenants, and making a steady, continuous effort to understand the full meaning. God speaks his word, and revelations come.

"The endowment is so richly symbolic that only a fool would attempt to describe it; it is so packed full of revelations to those who exercise their strength to seek and see, that no human works can explain or make clear the possibilities that reside in the temple service. The endowment, which was given by revelation, can best be understood by revelation; and to those who seek most vigorously, with pure hearts, will the revelation be the greatest.

"I believe that the busy person on the farm, in the shop, in the office, or in the household, who has his worries and troubles, can solve his problems better and more quickly in the house of the Lord than anywhere else. If he will leave his problems behind and do the temple work for himself and for the dead, he will confer a mighty blessing upon those who have gone before and quite as large a blessing will come to him; for at the most unexpected moments, in or out of the temple, will come to him, as a revelation, the solution of the problems that vex his life. That is the gift that comes to those who enter the temple properly, because it is a place where revelations may be expected. I bear you my personal testimony that this is so."

Temples and Temple Work

In early morning seminary class this past week, the instructor asked for a definition of "conversion." There were a number of responses, and then I added that for me, conversion was an "ongoing process." Sometimes it was realizing that I already knew something was true all along. Occasionally, it was learning something new and having the Holy Spirit witness to me with a burning in my heart. Often it was a reconfirmation of a profound truth. Finally, and most often, it occurs when I seek after something and then find it.

Heavenly Father has given us temples to help us in our eternal, ongoing conversion process. In his Holy House, we receive eternal ordinances, and we are endowed with power and knowledge that is essential for us to enter God's presence and to have eternal increase. It is there that we learn a higher form of love as we serve by providing these same blessings for those dead we do not know and cannot see. We also are allowed to retreat to these inspiring sacred places to receive personal revelation in dealing with the challenges of everyday living.

In the temple, I discovered that I knew all my life that temple work was true and right. As a child, I remember my mother ironing temple clothes each week before my parents would leave us to go to the temple. In my simple mind, I imagined my mother would be handing my father bricks or tools as they worked. She would be giving him a cool glass of water, as I had seen her do so many times while working in the yard. But, she explained that they were doing baptisms, endowments, and sealings for the dead. In my imagination, I could not figure out how that could be done for so many dead bodies rotting in the earth. She explained that it was done vicariously for them as they waited in spirit on the other side of the veil.

I have that same vision in my mind today as my mother explained temple work. It has always been easy for me to explain the words endowment, sealing, or vicarious work to people of other churches who don't understand or believe. I simply repeat what my mother told me as a child and explain that Christ performed a vicarious work for all of mankind when he suffered and died for us on the cross. Yesterday, while testing my own children's understanding, I explained it all—and then my six-year-old daughter asked, "Daddy, can you touch the ceilings in the temple or are they too high?" That leaves something to be desired about my ability to teach. I explained the whole thing a second time.

Temples and Truth

In the temple, I have learned some profound truths. These are a few that might be appropriate to share in public:

While working in the Washington D.C. Temple it was made known to me that people on the other side of the veil are just as willing and anxious to help us as we are to help them. There are indeed ministering angels! Sometimes these ministering angels are our own ancestors, or our departed friends, or even our descendants yet unborn. I testify of their influence in our lives.

Another profound truth I learned in the temple is that our spouses and our children are the most important investigators of the Gospel that we will ever be privileged to teach. I testify of this!

On another occasion, it was revealed to me that our journals and our life histories will be read by our descendants for many generations into the millennium. When they read about these last days as we are preparing for the Second Coming of our Lord Jesus Christ, our experiences will be a necessary and sustaining influence in their lives that we cannot really understand.

My Father's Work in the Temple

For example, I would like to tell you about my father's work in the temple. He just had his 90th birthday in June. He was born in a log home in Idaho and has seen the first automobiles come and go. He watched the first man walk on the moon. During almost a century of living, he has seen many wars, along with many other signs of the times. He has reared ten children and has over fifty grandchildren and over seventy great-grandchildren. Today, we all revere him as a great patriarch and leader of our family. During the millennium, his descendants will read in our journals about his dedication to temple work. For example, in the month of March in 1983, he did 101 endowment sessions—in one month!!! And almost 1,000 for that year.

True, he lives close to a temple and only needed to drive less than an hour. But his descendants will also read about the Peruvian families who had to travel for days on buses and trains to get to the Lima Temple. Because they were so poor, they had to choose which of their children could go with them to be sealed and which had to be left behind. They lacked money enough to take their large family on the trip. My heart melts at the thought of them.

May we do our part of the work, be edified in the process, receive revelation, and leave a heritage to inspire our children and our children's children.

35.

TESTIMONY

The Debate

In the November 1899 issue of *The Improvement Era* (the predecessor of the *Ensign magazine*) there is an account of an elder who accepted the invitation to debate a local minister before a large group. When the minister began, he criticized the elder and asked, "How do you know all this so surely? Do you know it by evidence of sight?" To each, the answer was "No."

"Then you know it only by the evidence of feeling. This young man says he knows beyond any doubt that Mormonism is the only true church; yet when we come to inquire, his assurance is based on the testimony of only one of the five senses—that of feeling!" Then the minister went on to elaborate on the absurdity of this claim.

The elder knew that he had to do something to strengthen his argument. So he bent a pin and placed it on the minister's chair. When the minister concluded his allotted time and sat down, he immediately rose again with an "Ouch!"

"What's the matter?" innocently asked the elder.

"You know very well," was the retort. "You put a pin on my seat!"

"Did you see it? Hear it? Taste or smell it?"

"You know I didn't, but I felt it!" protested the minister.

The elder turned to the audience and said, "Here is a man who would have us believe that he knows that I put a pin on his chair, when he has only the evidence of a just one of the five senses."

The elder continued with his message and teaching the importance of knowing by spiritually feeling the Holy Ghost.

I testify to you that I know that God lives, Jesus is the Christ, and he has revealed the truth of his Gospel to us in these latter days through living prophets.

Arabian Proverb

When I was a new missionary in New England, President Boyd K. Packer, shared the following Arabian proverb at one of my first zone conferences. Since then, I have also heard it called a Spanish or Chinese proverb. It goes like this:

He who knows not and knows not that he knows not, He is a fool, shun him.

He who knows not and knows that he knows not, He is simple, teach him.

He who knows and knows not that he knows, He is asleep, wake him.

He who knows and knows that he knows, He is wise, follow him.

Power of Testimony

President Packer then taught us many things about the importance and power of testimony. He taught us that the converting power of the Gospel lies in the testimony born by church members or missionaries to their friends, investigators or to one another. The same applies when we teach our companions or spouses, or our children.

"For when a man speaketh by the power of the Holy Ghost, the power of the Holy Ghost carrieth it into the hearts of the children of men" (2 Nephi 32:1).

A Talk May Not Be a Testimony

He explained that we are not testifying when we just tell about how we came to get a testimony, express gratitude, exhort, admonish, or discuss Gospel principles. When we tell others about the church or teach Gospel principles, it becomes easy to tell *about* our testimony without bearing a personal witness of the truth.

Two Ways to Spell a Word

The commonly used word to bear a testimony is spelled "b e a r." According to the dictionary, it means: 1) To carry; 2) To have or to show (as it bore his signature); 3) To support or sustain; and 4) To supply (as to bear witness). The other spelling is "b a r e" which means to expose or to make known or visible; to reveal or uncover. We all carry (bear) a testimony where ever we go and whatever we do. We should also concentrate on uncovering; revealing and making visible (bare) our testimony.

The Book of Mormon Gives Direct Witness

The Book of Mormon is a powerful witness of Jesus Christ because it gives direct testimony to the reader. In the book, the words "I know" are used in testimony 101 times, in addition to being used over 700 times relating to knowledge. Alma 5: 45 and 46 is a good example:

"And this is not all. Do ye not suppose that I know of these things myself? Behold, I testify unto you that I do know that these things whereof I have spoken are true. And how do ye suppose that I know of their surety?

"Behold, I say unto you they are made known unto me by the Holy Spirit of God. Behold, I have fasted and prayed many days that I might know these things of myself. And now I do know of myself that they are true; for the Lord God hath made them manifest unto me by his Holy Spirit; and this is the spirit of revelation which is in me."

Begin with What You Know

Begin by presenting a direct testimony of truths, such as: We lived before we were born; God is our father; We are here to gain a body and be tested; Jesus is the Christ, the Savior and Redeemer of the world; Jesus established his church; Jesus was the first to be resurrected; There was an apostasy; The Father and Son appeared to Joseph Smith; the church was restored; Living apostles and prophets are on the earth today; Priesthood holders are authorized servants to teach and baptize; The Church of Jesus Christ of Latter-day Saints is his church.

An Act of Faith

President Packer encouraged us to "Bear testimony of the things that you *hope* are true. Do it as an act of faith, even though you may not know for certain that they are true. You will find in the process of bearing your testimony that the confirmation will come to you that the principles are true. And, you will know as you bear it that you speak the truth. Then will come to you the greatest experience of bearing witness under the power of the Spirit. You will testify of things that you have believed in and hoped for and only now, in the bearing of them, do you know for certain that they are true. Then you will feel the Spirit speaking through you."

My son, Jonathan, recently wrote from Venezuela describing a "horrible, but great" evening when teaching some investigators in a member's home. He said that the discussion went very badly as their investigators argued over every point. He just wanted to leave, as the Spirit had left them. He bowed his head and prayed. When things were at their lowest, he indicated for his companion to stop talking. He began to bear his testimony and said that he went on faith. "When I bore my testimony this night about the Book of Mormon that I knew it was true, the Spirit hit me so strong, I felt that awesome feeling you can't deny . . . I felt the Spirit so strong. The Lord helped me this night with my testimony . . ."

I wrote to him and told him that perhaps in years to come, he would look back on this special conversion experience and his increase in the strength of testimony as one of the highlights of his mission experience. I encouraged him to share this blessing to strengthen other missionaries.

President Hinckley Speaks on Testimony

During General Conference, President Gordon B. Hinckley expressed his gratitude to the Lord for many things, including the faith, prayers, obedience and support of the members and youth. But most of all he was grateful for his testimony of Jesus Christ. He reported that on one occasion a missionary had asked him to "Give us your testimony, and tell us how you gained it." President Hinckley then told three stories describing the development of his testimony. The first was when he was five years old and received a priesthood blessing to heal the pain of an earache. The second was remembering getting into a warm bed in their cold bedroom and thinking of the significance of what he had just done in speaking to his Father in Heaven in prayer.

The third was describing how he and his missionary companion would read the Gospel of John and discuss each passage. He said, "Jesus went about Galilee, Samaria, and Judea preaching the Gospel of salvation, causing the blind to see, the lame to walk, the dead to rise to life again. And then, to fulfill his Father's plan of happiness for his children, He gave his life as a price for the sins of each of us."

Finally, President Hinckley attributed the growth of his testimony to the reading of the Book of Mormon. He bore testimony that "Jesus is my friend. He is my exemplar. He is my teacher. He is my healer. He is my leader, my Savior, and my Redeemer. Those who walked with him in Palestine bore witness of his divinity. The centurion who watched him die declared in solemnity, 'Truly this was the Son of God' (Matthew 24:54).

"And the Prophet Joseph, speaking in this dispensation, declared: 'And now, after the many testimonies which have been given of him, this is the testimony, last of all, which we give of him: That he lives! For we saw him, even on the right hand of God; and we heard the voice bearing record that he is the Only Begotten of the Father'" (D&C 76:22-23).

Warn Your Neighbor

"Behold, I sent you out to testify and warn the people, and it becometh every man who hath been warned to warn his neighbor" (D&C 88:81). I testify that you and I are on the Lord's errand and we are giving light and truth to others, one testimony at a time.

A Heritage of Sacrifice

At times in our teachings we emphasize some of the more attractive or acceptable principles of the Gospel and tend to avoid those which require great sacrifice. Such is the case many times when we teach our investigators or members about the principles of tithing or the Word of Wisdom.

In a mission president's seminar, Elder Dallin H. Oaks challenged us to help the Peruvian people develop a "Heritage of Sacrifice." He shared the following account about one of his ancestors:

"We draw strength and determination because of the sacrifices of our pioneer forefathers. . . . To all members in the world, and those in this part of the world, I say, 'Build your traditions of sacrifice so that your children can draw strength from your sacrifices.' Help the church leaders in South America to think how they, too, can build this heritage of sacrifice.

"I would like to tell you a story in my life. My great-grandfather from England, whose name was Justice Wellington Seely, had three sons. David was faithful and mature, as were John and Orange. Many times they were called by the prophet Joseph Smith and Brigham Young to move, first from Kirtland to Missouri, then to Nauvoo, and then to Salt Lake City and Pleasant Grove. One of the final moves that David was asked to make by Brigham Young was to go to San Bernardino, California, to establish a saw mill and an outlet to the sea for the Mormon colonies in the mountains there. David, his wife and children, and his brothers, John and Orange, left in approximately 1852-1854 and went to San Bernardino. They had, once again, given up everything.

"During that time the United States government sent Johnson's Army to Utah to put down the 'Mormon Rebellion.' Later, Brigham Young sent word that David Seely and his brothers were to return to Utah. David, John, and Orange, with their wagons and horses, were all ready to leave when John's wife said, 'I've made my last move for Brigham Young!'

"This was a very troubling time for John. His wife would not return with him. So he rode for two and a half months over 800 miles with his brothers to Pleasant Grove. Then John went on to Salt Lake City to see Brigham Young. He asked, 'What should I do?' The answer was, 'Your place is with your wife. Go and be with her.' John did, but sadly, within one generation there was not one active member of the church in the John Seely line.

"Orange returned to Utah, to Pleasant Grove, and later met Hanna, a Swedish immigrant recently off the trail. He saw her and immediately fell in love with her. They were soon married. They were later asked to go over the mountains to Emery County to settle. Even today it is difficult to go over the mountains to Emery County. What great strength! I know that my great-grandfather would go anywhere the prophet asked him to go. To the last of his life he was faithful."

In summary, Elder Oaks said, "I have a personal testimony because I studied the Gospel and read the Book of Mormon. I prayed and attended church, and the Holy Ghost has born witness that it is true. But the reason *I am faithful* is because they were faithful! Teach your people to develop this heritage of sacrifice."

We, Too, Are Sacrificing

As missionaries, we too are sacrificing. We must remember the sacred covenants we have made with the Lord. We must remember that all that we have comes from him, and all that we have is for the building up of the Kingdom of God.

There is a problem when a missionary thinks or says, "This is my life or my time and this is my money. I will spend it how I like and no one should tell me what to do." Perhaps that missionary is forgetting that we are on this mission to do the Lord's work and to do it the Lord's way. President Loren C. Dunn shared the following experience he had with such a missionary:

"On my first assignment to tour a mission, a discouraged mission president asked if I would take a few minutes to talk to one of his problem missionaries. The mission president explained that the young man was one of the most successful missionaries in baptizing, but that he broke all the rules. I found him almost flippantly saying that he was doing all that was expected of him. He was baptizing people. That is what he was sent to do, and he was doing it. He had the attitude that he just wanted to be left alone to live the way he wanted to.

"During that interview the spirit of the Lord placed in my mind something that I had not thought before. I asked this young missionary if he did not understand that disobedient, uncommitted missionaries will baptize disobedient and uncommitted members."

We teach what we are. We receive blessings through obedience. As we teach principles such as sacrifice, tithing, and the Word of Wisdom, we can teach our investigators and members with great enthusiasm and assurance that they will receive great blessings by obedience.

Living the Word of Wisdom is often a great sacrifice for new members, who find it very difficult to give up their tobacco, coffee, or alcohol. However, as I think of the great promises attached to these commandments, I desire to immediately share them with everyone. For example, we read in D&C 89:18-21 the promises made to those who live the Word of Wisdom and also obey the commandments of God. Originally, it was given as a "principle with a promise" and later became a commandment. Who would not want all of these blessings? Who would not be willing to sacrifice to obtain them if they but knew the promise of the Lord?

When we pay our tithes and offerings we are blessed in abundance. The opposite is also true. You as individuals and the whole nation are under a curse when you do *not* pay your tithes and offerings. The devourer will consume all that you have through sickness, war, famine, unemployment, inflation, and a multitude of other ways. The answer is to sacrifice and to pay your tithing.

As we read in D&C 64: 23, 33-34:

"Behold, now it is called today until the coming of the son of Man, and verily it is a day of sacrifice and for the tithing of my people; for he that is tithed shall not be burned at his coming.

"Wherefore, be not weary in well-doing, for ye are laying the foundation of a great work. And out of small things proceedeth that which is great.

"Behold, the Lord requireth the heart and a willing mind; and the willing and obedient shall eat the good of the land of Zion in these last days."

His is the promise of the Lord to you. This is my promise to you.

36.

UNITY AND LOVE

Teamwork and collaboration allow common people to achieve uncommon results. As members of the Gospel of Christ, our hearts need to be knit together as one. "If ye are not one, ye are not mine" (D&C 38:27). We desire harmony so we can move in the same direction at the same time.

I once asked a missionary under my direction what he thought was most needed to increase the effectiveness of our mission. His response was that we needed more love. This was Elder Severino, serving in the program of San Geronimo in Cuzco. He and his companion showed great love and unity in their companionship, which was one of the reasons for their success.

One of the effects of love is unity. We read in the New Testament that we in the church should be of one mind, "Finally, brethren, Farewell. Be perfect, be of good comfort, *be of one mind*, live in peace; and the God of love and peace shall be with you" (2 Cor. 13:11).

In Philippians 1:27 we learn that we should be firm and of the same spirit: "Only let your conversation be as it becometh the Gospel of Christ: that whether I come and see you, or else be absent, I may hear of your affairs, *that ye stand fast in one spirit, with one mind striving together* for the faith of the Gospel."

And then, regarding the ancient inhabitants in the city of Enoch, we read, "And the Lord called his people Zion, because *they were of one heart and one mind*, and dwelt in righteousness: and there was no poor among them" (Moses 7:18).

We know that love is the greatest commandment, and we know that by loving God, ourselves, and others we will develop a unity and spirit among us that will help us to truly become Zion. It is my prayer that we can unitedly work toward this goal. I give this invitation and challenge to one and all.

37.

WOMEN OF MY LIFE

Woman change the course of history by helping men change for the better. I would like to introduce you to the women of my life who have helped me and have been a powerful influence in the world.

My great-great-grandmother, Kristine Christensen, did not join the LDS church, but consented to her husband and four children to be baptized and come to Utah in 1860, while she stayed behind in her native land of Denmark. Her son, Niels, lived in a cave during his first year in Hyrum, Utah. He married my great-grandmother, Karen Hansen, who reared eight children in very difficult circumstances, but kept the faith during it all.

Her oldest son, Christian, became a cowboy in Wyoming and was later the constable of Cache County. He married my grandmother, a Norwegian girl named Bena Maria Frogner, who later lost some of her hearing to typhoid fever. While she lost one of her eight babies to an early death, she never lost one of her children to inactivity in the church. They all served the Lord, and were all faithful missionaries. She activated my cowboy grandfather and got them to the temple before they moved to Goshen, Idaho, where my father was born in a small log cabin in 1899.

My father was one of only 200+ missionaries to serve a mission during the first part of the World War I era. My grandmother lived close to the Spirit and began a tradition of missionary work that lives on in the lives of her descendants to this day. Hundreds of her descendants have been endowed and sealed in the temple and served faithful missions to share the Gospel throughout the earth.

Esther Swift, my great-grandmother on my mother's side of the family, and her daughter, Esther, were the first in their families to accept the LDS Gospel in Yorkshire, England. They hosted many apostles, missionaries, and traveling church leaders in their home. They both waited patiently for my great-grandfather to accept the Gospel and be baptized.

My grandmother, Esther Thornton, married a new convert to the LDS Church, and immigrated to Utah. She raised a large family of six daughters and two sons. Some served missions while others served their country in war time. Many hundreds of her descendants have been blessed with sacred temple covenants and have served missions and shared the Gospel with countless others. Esther sent her husband off on five full-time missions and three stake missions. She stayed at home to raise her children, tend the family store, garden, and raise small animals to provide for the family. When her husband returned from his missions, she often introduced him to a new daughter or son. In her later years, she did a lot of genealogical and temple work and served a full-time mission with my grandfather in England right after World War II. They were one of the first missionary couples. She had great faith, and on one occasion experienced the miracle of the loaves and the fishes in feeding many guests in their tiny flat.

My mother, Esther Christensen, served a full-time mission and then married my father, a widower, who already had five growing children. She bore him five more children. She sacrificed many of the nice things of the world in order to move to Idaho and become the wife of a teacher and farmer. As a young mother, she endured great physical illness, but lived into her late nineties. She taught her children love and repentance and was always there as a gentle reminder to be valiant. When I left home for the first time to catch the midnight train from Blackfoot, Idaho, to New York City, and on to London, England, she slipped a note in my hand, reminding me to remain morally clean.

My sisters all supported all their sons on missions. Two of them also served with their husbands as missionary couples. My daughter Teresa served a mission in the Texas Dallas Mission, and another daughter, Tamara, served in the Japan Hiroshima mission.

Along with my relatives, I want to mention Patricia Hoge, Susie Wear, Cynthia Carlson and Sharon Gardner and Carla Smith who were my high school and college girlfriends who inspired me to be my best, to be true, prepare for and serve an honorable mission. Even though I was born into the church, they served as my missionaries who helped me in my conversion during my early years. Also, my many Primary and Sunday school teachers, mothers of my friends, sisters of the wards I've lived in etc. I can't tell you how powerfully they have changed the world for the better.

Finally, I pay tribute to my dear wife, Mary-Jo, who has been a great missionary since she was baptized at nineteen years of age. She was the first convert in her family. She served as my missionary companion during our mission in Peru and continues to inspire me and our family as she perpetuates the missionary zeal of a disciple of Christ. I know that because of her, our children, grandchildren, and great-grandchildren will be faithful and share the Gospel with others. That's just who she is and what she does.

38.

WORK, PERSONAL RESPONSIBILITY, AND JOY

The Doctrine of Work

"Let us realize that the privilege to work is a gift, that the power to work is a blessing, that the love of work is success."
--David 0. McKay

"Work is a blessing from God. It is a fundamental principle of salvation, both spiritual and temporal. . . . We are co-creators with God. He gave us the capacity to do the work he left undone, to harness the energy, mine the ore, and use the treasures of the earth for our good. But most important, the Lord knew that from the crucible of work emerges the hard core of character." --J. Richard Clarke

"We have a moral obligation to exercise our personal capabilities of mind, muscle, and spirit in a way that will return to the Lord, our families, and our society the fruits of our best efforts. To do less is to live our lives unfulfilled. It is to deny ourselves and those dependent upon us opportunity and advantage.

"We work to earn a living, it is true; but as we toil, let us also remember that we are building a life. Our work determines what that life will be. . . . Work is honorable. It is a good therapy for most problems. Work is the antidote for worry. It is the equalizer for deficiency of native endowment. Work makes it possible for the average to approach genius. What we may lack in aptitude, we can make up for in performance." --J. Richard Clarke

Rest on the Sabbath

It is also important to take a day off from work. This day will renew your energy and your mental outlook. Work for six days and rest on the seventh. This is a day appointed to rest from labors. Exodus 20:9-11 says: " Six days shalt thou labor, and do all thy work: But the seventh day is the Sabbath of the LORD thy God: in it thou shalt not do any work, thou, nor thy son, nor thy daughter, thy manservant, nor thy maidservant, nor thy cattle, nor thy stranger that is within thy gates: For in six days the LORD made heaven and earth, the sea, and all that in them is, and rested the seventh day: wherefore the LORD blessed the Sabbath day, and hallowed it."

The Sabbath day is also to be used to worship God. D&C 59:9 explains this: "And that thou mayest more fully keep thyself unspotted from the world, thou shalt go to the house of prayer and offer up thy sacraments upon my holy day . . . For verily this is a day appointed unto you to rest from your labors, and to pay thy devotions unto the Most High . . . Nevertheless thy vows shall be offered up in righteousness on all days and at all times . . . But remember that on this, the Lord's day, thou shalt offer thine oblations and thy sacraments unto the Most High, confessing thy sins unto thy brethren, and before the Lord."

Parable of the Talents

The parable of the talents shows the importance of working wisely. It is told in Matthew 25:14-30:

14 For the kingdom of heaven is as a man travelling into a far country, who called his own servants, and delivered unto them his goods.

15 And unto one he gave five talents, to another two, and to another one; to every man according to his several ability; and straightway took his journey.

16 Then he that had received the five talents went and traded with the same, and made them other five talents.

17 And likewise he that had received two, he also gained other two.

18 But he that had received one went and digged in the earth, and hid his lord's money.

19 After a long time the lord of those servants cometh, and reckoneth with them.

20 And so he that had received five talents came and brought other five talents, saying, Lord, thou deliverdest unto me five talents: behold, I have gained beside them five talents more.

21 His lord said unto him, Well done, thou good and faithful servant: thou hast been faithful over a few things, I will make thee ruler over many things: enter thou into the joy of thy lord.

22 He also that had received two talents came and said, Lord, thou deliveredst unto me two talents: behold, I have gained two other talents beside them.

23 His lord said unto him, Well done, good and faithful servant; thou hast been faithful over a few things, I will make thee ruler over many things: enter thou into the joy of thy lord.

24 Then he which had received the one talent came and said, Lord, I knew thee that thou art an hard man, reaping where thou hast not sown, and gathering where thou hast not strawed:

25 And I was afraid, and went and hid thy talent in the earth: lo, there thou hast that is thine.

26 His lord answered and said unto him, Thou wicked and slothful servant, thou knewest that I reap where I sowed not, and gather where I have not strawed:

27 Thou oughtest therefore to have put my money to the exchangers, and then at my coming I should have received mine own with usury.

28 Take therefore the talent from him, and give it unto him which hath ten talents.

29 For unto every one that hath shall be given, and he shall have abundance: but from him that hath not shall be taken away even that which he hath.

30 And cast ye the unprofitable servant into outer darkness: there shall be weeping and gnashing of teeth.

Scriptural Guides

I Thessalonians *4:11-12:* "And that ye study to be quiet, and to do your own business, and to work with your own hands, as we commanded you . . . That ye may walk honestly toward them that are without, and that ye may have lack of nothing."

I Timothy 5:8: "But if any provide not for his own, and especially for those of his own house, he hath denied the faith, and is worse than an infidel."

2 Nephi 5:17: "And it came to pass that I, Nephi, did cause my people to be industrious, and to labor with their hands."

D&C 60:13: "Thou shalt not idle away thy time, neither shalt thou bury thy talent."

Moses 5:1: "And it came to pass that after I, the Lord God, had driven them out, that Adam began to till the earth, and to have dominion over all the beasts of the field, and to eat his bread by the sweat of his brow, as I the Lord had commanded him. And Eve, also, his wife, did labor with him."

Quotes on Work

"If you are poor, work. If you are happy, work. Idleness gives room for doubts and fears. If disappointments come, keep right on working. If sorrow overwhelms you, work. When faith falters and reason fails, just work. When dreams are shattered and hope seems dead, work. Work as if your life were in peril. It really is. No matter what ails you, work. Work faithfully. Work is the greatest remedy available for both mental and physical afflictions." --Korsaren, *The Forbes Scrapbook of Thoughts on the Business of Life*

"The happiest man is he who has toiled hard and successfully in his life work. The work may be done in a thousand different ways; with the brain or the hands, in the study, the field, or in the workshop; if it is honest work, honestly done and well worth doing; that is all we have a right to ask." -- Theodore Roosevelt

"... As Latter-day Saints, if we would be true to our religion, we must perform high-quality work. It is a matter of integrity. Every piece of work we do is a portrait of the one who produced it. We are increasingly concerned with the diminishing quality of work in our society. On every hand we see shoddy workmanship for which full compensation is expected, whether the product meets acceptable standards or not. We must be motivated by a higher ideal than simply meeting the artificial standard of a society, which has allowed inferior performance to be acceptable. That is not the Mormon ethic. In times of unemployment, Latter-day Saints who practice the work principles of our religion should be in great demand." --J. Richard Clarke, *The Value of Work*

Full and Honest Effort

Let us give full, honest effort to our jobs as though we owned the enterprise. In a very real sense, each of us is in business for ourselves, no matter who pays us. Be honest with your employer. Make sure that "the laborer is worthy of his hire" (D&C 84:79).

Our employers should get the best we have in us, not just enough to get by or to meet common standards. Each of us should set a personal standard based upon our ability. Let us exemplify the old motto: A Full Day's Work for a Full Day's Pay.

Continue to invest in your personal development. Expand your occupational horizons by constant study. Use your spare time wisely. If we waste thirteen minutes each day, it is the equivalent of two weeks a year without pay. Look to your present job as a stepping-stone along your career path.

Take time to think. The dimensions of most jobs are constrained only by the mind of the uncreative worker. I like what one businessman counseled: "If at first you do succeed, try something harder!"

Teaching our children to work is a primary duty of parenthood. Our children have experienced unprecedented prosperity created by parents who have worked hard to provide what they, themselves, did not have as children. If we are to save our children temporally and spiritually, we must train them to work. They must learn by example that work is not drudgery, but a blessing. Fortunate is the young man or woman who has learned how to work. Wise is the parent who requires children to lean responsibility and to meet acceptable performance standards.

Leisure vs. Idleness

Now, what about our leisure time? How we use our leisure is equally as important to our joy as our occupational pursuits. Proper use of leisure requires discriminating judgment. Our leisure provides opportunity for renewal of spirit, mind, and body. It is a time for worship, for family, for service, for study, for wholesome recreation. It brings harmony into our life.

Leisure is not idleness. The Lord condemns idleness. He said, "Thou shalt not idle away thy time, neither shalt thou bury thy talent" (D&C 60:13). Idleness in any form produces boredom, conflict, and unhappiness. It creates a vacancy of worth, a seedbed for mischief and evil. It is the enemy of progress and salvation.

The individual is all-important in the Lord's plan. Any system which does not require initiative, self-reliance, and the necessity of work for what we receive, if able, will not preserve the integrity of the individual.

D&C 75:29 says: "Let every man be diligent in all things. And the idler shall not have place in the church, except he repent and mend his ways."

Brigham Young declared, "It is never any benefit to give out . . . to man or woman, money, food, clothing, or anything else, if they are able-bodied, and can work and earn what they need. To give to the idler is as wicked as anything else. Never give anything to the idler. Set the poor to work." *--Discourses of Brigham Young*

In the broader sense, work is the means to achieve happiness, prosperity, and salvation. When work, duty, and joy are co-mingled, then people are at their best.

Tagore wrote, "I slept and dreamt, That life was joy. I woke and saw, That life was duty. I acted, and behold! Duty was joy!" --Quoted by Earl Nightingale, *Our Changing World*

About the Author

The author, Dale Christensen, received an MBA from Boston College in 1975 and has had valuable experience in several industries throughout his professional career. He has authored several books, including:

The Shopping Center Acquisition Handbook (1984)
Turning the Hearts (Vol. 1-4, 1983-8)
Thoughts in Verse (1982, 2001, 2005, & 2014)
Entrepreneur's Guide: The Ultimate Business & Learning Experience (2001)
10 Secrets to Speaking English (2001)
A Disciple's Journey (2014)
Patriot's Path (2014)
Dark Horse Candidate (2014).

Dale has also written numerous business-related newspaper articles and is a popular public speaker. He wants to make a difference in people's lives so they will make a difference in the world. He wants to motivate others to apply what they have learned in order to make the world a better place. He wants to be a great teacher and teach others to be the same.

www.ingramcontent.com/pod-product-compliance
Lightning Source LLC
Chambersburg PA
CBHW052032090426
42739CB00010B/1882
* 9 7 8 1 9 4 2 3 4 5 1 3 8 *